Privacy Tools in the Age of AI: Practical Strategies with VPNs, Secure DNS, Private Relay and Intelligent Defenses

ISBN 979-8991776295

party for any loss, damage, or disruption caused by errors or omissions, whether such errors or omissions result from negligence, accident, or any other cause.

Contents

1 Introduction

Privacy and security online have never been more important in the age of artificial intelligence (AI). In today's interconnected world, many facets of our digital lives—browsing habits, location, device information, and even personal data—can be tracked or exploited. This book provides **comprehensive, practical guidance** on protecting your privacy using modern tools. We cover everything from VPNs and encrypted DNS to browser hardening and the latest platform features (like Apple's iCloud Private Relay and AI privacy). Throughout, we include step-by-step tutorials, comparison tables, and code examples for both GUI and CLI setups on Windows, macOS, Linux, Android, and iOS. By the end, you'll have a deep understanding of how to build a robust privacy "stack" and the know-how to configure it.

Why digital privacy matters: Every time you go online, your device communicates with servers around the world—every web query, login, or download leaves a trace. Internet service providers (ISPs), websites, ad networks, and even malicious actors can log this activity. A standard DNS lookup, for example, can reveal every site you visit (IP addresses and hostnames). Without protection, your browsing history can be logged, analyzed, or sold. In some regions, ISPs are legally required to keep logs of user activity. Even in secure encrypted connections, metadata like the destination IP and hostname can leak information. Our goal is to **limit what information is exposed**. We use encryption (VPNs, TLS, encrypted DNS) to hide traffic, anonymization tools (e.g. Tor)

1

to conceal identity, and device/browser settings to minimize tracking. This defense-in-depth approach assumes no single tool is perfect, but together they greatly improve your privacy.

Threat model and principles: Who might be watching you? It could be your ISP, big tech companies, governments, or hackers. Each may have different capabilities (passive monitoring, active interference, strong legal authority, etc.). We assume worst-case: Attackers could intercept your internet traffic or run DNS servers. We also assume you trust some providers (like Cloudflare or Apple) only to a point. Key principles include *encrypt all sensitive traffic, avoid logging, minimize data collection*, and *separate identity from activity*. For example, a VPN can hide your IP from websites, but you must trust the VPN provider not to log your usage. Apple's iCloud Private Relay tries to split trust by using two relays (so no single entity knows both your identity and what you're browsing). We'll see many such trade-offs.

Throughout this book, we use a step-by-step format. Important terms are introduced in context. Configuration and code examples are marked with code blocks, and comparison tables help summarize choices. In Chapter 2, we'll get started with fundamentals of network privacy and threats.

2 Fundamentals of Network Privacy and Threats

Privacy starts with understanding what data your device sends out, and what can be observed or logged. Every internet request involves DNS lookups, connecting to IP addresses, and sending packets that include unencrypted metadata.

- **DNS and visibility:** Normally, when you type an internet address, your device sends a DNS query (often in plaintext) to a resolver (usually your ISP or a public DNS). *This reveals the exact domain names you are visiting*, which an observer can log. Without protection, a network eavesdropper sees every domain query and the IP connections from your device.

- **IP address tracking:** Your public IP address (assigned by your ISP) ties all your activity to you. It can reveal your approximate location and ISP. Websites and trackers often log IPs in their access logs. If someone can link your IP to your identity (e.g. via ISP records), they know which sites you visit.

- **Traffic metadata:** Even if you use HTTPS, which encrypts content, an observer sees *which IP addresses you connect to* and *when*. The content is hidden, but patterns remain (e.g. you contacted `1.1.1.1` which is Cloudflare).

- **Device and application fingerprinting:** Browsers and mobile apps expose many details (user agent, installed fonts, screen size, etc.) that can uniquely identify

3

you (a "fingerprint"). This allows tracking across sessions if not mitigated.

- **Cross-device correlation:** Using the same login or accounts across devices means an adversary can link your mobile, desktop, and other activity together.

Important terms and acronyms:

Below are clear, concise definitions of the key terms and acronyms that appear in this book. Use this as a quick reference while reading the rest of the book.

1. **DNS:** Domain Name System. The internet's "phonebook" that translates human-friendly domain names (like example.com) into numeric IP addresses that computers use to route traffic.

2. **DNS lookup:** The actual query your device sends to a DNS resolver asking "what is the IP address for <domain name>?" In default (unencrypted) DNS, these lookups are visible to anyone observing the network.

3. **IP address:** Internet Protocol address. A numeric identifier assigned to a device or server on a network (e.g., 192.0.2.1). A public IP exposes your approximate location and which ISP you are using.

4. **ISP:** Internet Service Provider. The company (e.g., your home broadband or mobile carrier) that provides you internet access. ISPs commonly see unencrypted traffic and DNS queries from their customers.

5. **Metadata:** Data about data. In networking, metadata includes information like which IP you connected to, the timing and size of transfers, and the DNS names you

queried.

6. **Traffic metadata:** The subset of metadata produced by network activity: timestamps, destination IPs, packet sizes, connection durations, and similar observable facts that can reveal habits or patterns even when the content is encrypted.

7. **Device and application fingerprinting:** A technique that collects many small data points (browser version, fonts, screen size, installed plugins, etc.) to create a unique "fingerprint" that can identify or track a device across sessions and sites.

8. **Cross-device correlation:** Linking activity from multiple devices (e.g., phone, laptop, tablet) to a single person or account, usually by shared logins, IP addresses, or other signals—enabling tracking across contexts.

9. **Threat model:** A description of who/what you're defending against and what they can do. Examples: local Wi-Fi eavesdroppers, your ISP, malicious websites, nation-state actors. A threat model guides which protections you need.

10. **End-to-end encryption (E2EE):** A security model where only the communicating endpoints (sender and receiver) can read message contents. Intermediaries (including service providers) cannot decrypt the content. Common in secure messaging (e.g., Signal).

11. **Network encryption:** Encryption that protects traffic while it traverses networks (e.g., VPN tunnels, TLS for HTTPS). It prevents on-path observers from reading

packet contents, though some metadata (like IPs) may still be visible depending on the setup.

12. **VPN:** Virtual Private Network. A service or technology that creates an encrypted "tunnel" between your device and a VPN server. It hides your true IP from destination sites and prevents local observers (like public Wi-Fi or ISPs) from seeing the contents or destinations of your traffic.

13. **Tunnel:** A colloquial term for an encrypted connection (e.g., a VPN tunnel) that encapsulates and protects your network traffic while it passes through an untrusted network.

14. **Encrypted DNS:** Any DNS method that prevents plaintext queries from being observed on the network. Common encrypted DNS approaches include DoH (DNS over HTTPS), DoT (DNS over TLS), and DNSCrypt.

15. **DoH:** DNS over HTTPS. DNS requests are sent inside normal HTTPS traffic (port 443), hiding them from passive observers and often from censoring intermediaries.

16. **DoT:** DNS over TLS. DNS requests are encrypted using TLS (typically port 853). Android's "Private DNS" uses DoT.

17. **DNSCrypt:** A protocol (and set of implementations) that signs and encrypts DNS traffic between a client and resolver. Tools like `dnscrypt-proxy` implement this.

18. **Tor:** The Onion Router. A volunteer-run network that routes traffic through multiple relays (usually three) to provide strong anonymity. Tor hides the origin IP from the destination and makes traffic correlation much harder, but is slower than VPNs.

19. **Anonymization:** Techniques used to reduce or remove identifying information so actions cannot be linked back to a specific person. Tor is an anonymization tool; other approaches (mix networks, proxies) aim for similar goals with different trade-offs.

20. **Split-trust / Split-trust service:** A design approach that separates knowledge among multiple parties so no single party can fully associate your identity with your activities. (Example: Apple's iCloud Private Relay uses two different relays so neither one can see both who you are and what you visited.)

21. **Firewall:** A system (software or hardware) that enforces rules about which network connections are allowed or blocked. Firewalls can be used to implement a VPN "kill switch" (block traffic if the VPN is down) or to restrict inbound/outbound access.

22. **NAT:** Network Address Translation. A technique used by routers to let many devices share a single public IP address. NAT hides internal (private) IP addresses from the internet, but traffic originating from your network can still reveal the router's public IP.

We construct **threat models** to decide what to defend against. For example, if you want to evade local network snooping on public Wi-Fi, a VPN or Tor is critical. If you're concerned about websites knowing your location and browsing, a VPN or Private Relay helps hide your IP, while anti-tracking browser extensions can prevent ad networks from profiting off cookies. There are trade-offs: Tor provides strong anonymity but at the cost of speed; VPNs are faster but require trusting a provider. Our approach will layer protections: encryption of DNS (so your ISP can't see your queries), VPN/relay for IP hiding, and browser hardening to reduce fingerprintability.

Privacy vs. Security: Although related, they are not the same. Security protects data from unauthorized access or modification (confidentiality, integrity) often via encryption (e.g. HTTPS, VPN). Privacy is about controlling what personal information is collected, how it is used, and who can link actions to you. This guide emphasizes both: using encryption to secure the channel and also choosing tools/policies that *minimize data collection and exposure* (such as "no-log" policies for VPNs/DNS).

Key concepts:

- **End-to-end encryption** protects content (e.g. HTTPS, Signal).

- **Network encryption** (VPN, Tor) hides your traffic from local observers.

- **Anonymization** (Tor, Tor Browser) adds anti-correlation via relays.

- **Split-trust services** like iCloud Private Relay separate data flows.

- **Encrypted DNS** (DoH/DoT/DNSCrypt) prevents DNS snooping.

- **Firewall/NAT** typically hides your internal network, but outbound requests can still reveal info.

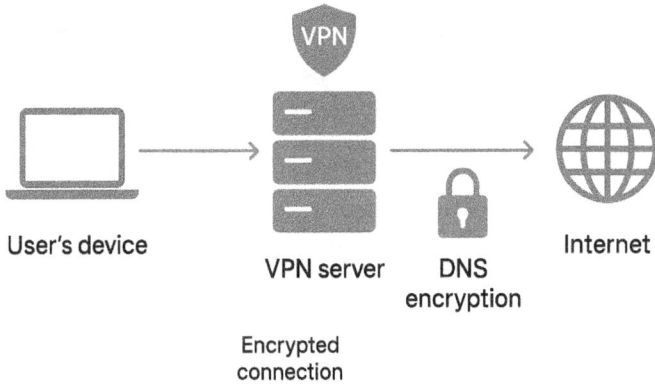

The figure above shows typical privacy tools in action. A VPN (or Private Relay) shields your IP and encrypts traffic, while encrypted DNS hides your DNS queries from onlookers.

3 Virtual Private Networks (VPNs)

A virtual private network (VPN) creates an encrypted tunnel between your device and a VPN server, hiding your traffic from local observers. As a result, the ISP sees only an encrypted connection to the VPN, not the final destinations you visit. Websites see the VPN's IP instead of yours, protecting your identity and location from them. In essence, a VPN moves trust from your ISP to the VPN provider.

3.1 VPN protocols overview

VPN tools use different protocols (tunneling technologies) to secure traffic. The main protocols today are **OpenVPN** (https://openvpn.net), **WireGuard** (https://wireguard.com) and **IKEv2/IPsec**. Older ones like **L2TP/IPsec**, **SSTP**, and **PPTP** exist but are generally deprecated (PPTP in particular is extremely insecure).

Here's a concise comparison:

Protocol	Security & Encryption	Speed & Performance
OpenVPN	Uses OpenSSL (typically AES-256), TCP/UDP transport. Very secure and open-source.	Moderate (UDP faster than TCP)
WireGuard	Modern crypto (ChaCha20, Poly1305), small	High (very fast)

Protocol	Security & Encryption	Speed & Performance
	codebase. Open-source. Only UDP.	
IKEv2/IPsec	Strong (IPsec), extremely stable rekeying. Supports MOBIKE for network changes.	High
L2TP/IPsec	Weak individually (L2TP no encryption); paired with IPsec.	Moderate
SSTP	Strong (SSL/TLS based, AES-256).	Moderate
PPTP	**Very weak** (MSMPPE with flawed MS-CHAP v1/v2).	Moderate
Others (Proprietary)	Example: NordLynx (WireGuard variant), Lightway (ExpressVPN, based on WireGuard).	Varies

Protocol	Best Use Cases	Notes
OpenVPN	General-purpose, widely supported,	Very mature; trusted by community; can be slower due to overhead.

Protocol	Best Use Cases	Notes
WireGuard	DIY connections High-speed needs (streaming, gaming, P2P)	Lightweight; requires storing recent IP on server (mitigated by RAM-only servers).
IKEv2/IPsec	Mobile devices (roaming networks)	Very fast to reconnect; open source implementations; closed-source origin (Cisco/Microsoft).
L2TP/IPsec	Legacy support, site-to-site links	Mostly obsolete; replaced by IKEv2/IPsec.
SSTP	Windows fallback	Windows-native, uses TCP 443; proprietary (MS).
PPTP	None (legacy only)	Not recommended. Very weak encryption.
Others (Proprietary)	Provider-specific features	Often marketing-driven; similar security to base protocol.

From a privacy standpoint, avoid PPTP and L2TP for public connections. WireGuard and OpenVPN are generally preferred due to strong crypto and transparency (open-source). IKEv2 is very fast, has strong crypto and is best for seamless connectivity on mobile devices.

OpenVPN has been around for ~25 years and is considered very secure. It supports AES-256 with OpenSSL and can run over TCP or UDP. UDP mode is faster (no acknowledgments) but less stable; TCP is slower but can pass through many firewalls. Client setup examples in section 3.6 will use the official OpenVPN Connect client for Windows, Android, and iOS, and Tunnelblick for macOS.

WireGuard (released 2016) is designed to be lean and fast. It has a small codebase (~4,000 lines, vs. 70k+ for OpenVPN), reducing attack surface. It uses a modern crypto suite (Curve25519, etc.) and achieves higher throughput. The trade-off: It by design keeps short-term IP addresses in memory for the connection, meaning if the server logs, it could tie you to an IP. Many privacy-minded services mitigate that by using RAM-only servers that auto-reset, wiping logs. In practice, WireGuard's speed gains (often ~50% faster than OpenVPN) and ease of configuration (simple keys) make it an excellent choice. Windows, macOS, Android and iOS all have official WireGuard clients; on Linux we'll use `wg-quick`.

IKEv2/IPsec is often built into devices. It's robust and fast, especially on mobile: It can re-establish a dropped connection automatically (when switching from Wi-Fi to cellular) with minimal interruption. It uses a combination of the IKEv2 protocol and IPsec encryption. IKEv2/IPsec is proprietary in origin, but the standard itself is widely implemented and open source (e.g. Libreswan, strongSwan).

Deprecated protocols: SSTP (Microsoft's SSL-based tunnel) is Windows-only and works but lacks broad support. PPTP is strongly discouraged: It's been broken by government agencies and others. If you see "PPTP" anywhere, avoid using it. L2TP/IPsec (L2TP over IPsec) is better than PPTP but can be blocked on some networks, use IKEv2/IPsec instead.

3.2 VPN comparison table

Protocol	Encryption	Use-case
OpenVPN (UDP/TCP)	AES-256 (OpenSSL), TLS 1.2/1.3	General use; when compatibility and security are needed
WireGuard	ChaCha20, Poly1305 (modern suite)	High-speed needs (streaming, gaming, P2P)
IKEv2/IPsec	IPsec (AES-256), IKEv2 key exchange	Mobile devices on-the-go (keeps VPN alive across networks)
L2TP/IPsec	256-bit IPsec, but L2TP adds overhead	Less used now; legacy setups
SSTP	SSL/TLS (AES-256)	Windows alternative if OpenVPN fails
PPTP	MPPE (weak RC4)	None (avoid)

Protocol	Strengths	Weaknesses
OpenVPN (UDP/TCP)	Proven secure, open-source, configurable (UDP/TCP)	More overhead (slower than WireGuard), complex config

14

Protocol	Strengths	Weaknesses
WireGuard	Simple, very fast, small codebase	Server stores IP briefly (mitigate with RAM-only servers)
IKEv2/IPsec	Fast reconnect (good for roaming), widely supported	Fixed ports (UDP 500/4500) can be filtered
L2TP/IPsec	Legacy compatibility on many devices	Often blocked by firewalls; extra overhead
SSTP	Works in Windows through TCP 443 (hard to block)	Windows-only, slower (TCP), proprietary
PPTP	Fast due to minimal encryption	Broken; not recommended

3.3 Choosing a VPN service

For advanced users, building your own VPN can be an effective way to enhance online privacy and security. Read the next section for more details. Others may find it easier to subscribe to a VPN service. Consider these important criteria when choosing a VPN service:

- **No-logs policy:** The provider should not record your browsing activity. Look for audited policies. Some, like Cloudflare's WARP or Mullvad (DNS/VPN), explicitly state no logs.

- **Jurisdiction:** Companies under certain countries' laws could be compelled to hand over data. E.g., a U.S.-based VPN must comply with subpoenas, although if they have a strict no-logs policy, they may have nothing to hand over.

- **Performance and server locations:** More servers worldwide means better speeds and more location options.

- **Multi-platform support:** GUI apps for Windows/macOS/Android/iOS, plus manual config for routers or Linux.

- **Kill switch:** Ability to block all network traffic if VPN disconnects, preventing unprotected leaks.

- **Protocols offered:** At minimum OpenVPN and WireGuard or IKEv2.

- **Additional features:** Split tunneling, double-hop (multi-hop) servers, built-in ad blockers, etc.

We won't endorse specific services here, but these guidelines will help you pick. In the next sections, we'll show how to build your own VPN server and how to configure VPN clients on your devices.

3.4 Building your own VPN

Building your own VPN can be an effective way to enhance online privacy and security while also providing flexibility and cost-effectiveness. With the right resources and guidance, it can be a valuable investment in your online security.

In this section, you'll learn how to build your own VPN server with WireGuard, OpenVPN and/or IPsec VPN with IKEv2. This is for **advanced users** only. If you prefer to subscribe to a VPN service instead, skip this section and go to section 3.5 Setting up WireGuard clients.

For more in-depth coverage of building your own VPN, please see my other books at https://amazon.com/author/linsong.

3.4.1 Create a cloud server

To build your own VPN, you will need a cloud server or virtual private server (VPS) as a first step. For your reference, here are some popular server providers:

- DigitalOcean (https://www.digitalocean.com)
- Vultr (https://www.vultr.com)
- Linode (https://www.linode.com)
- OVH (https://www.ovhcloud.com/en/vps/)

First, choose a server provider. Then refer to the example steps in this section to get started. When creating your server, it is recommended to select the latest Ubuntu Linux LTS or Debian Linux (Ubuntu 24.04 or Debian 13 at the time of writing) as the operating system, with 1 GB or more memory.

Advanced users can set up the VPN server on a Raspberry Pi (https://raspberrypi.com). First log in to your Raspberry Pi and open Terminal, then follow the instructions in this chapter to install OpenVPN, WireGuard and/or IPsec VPN with IKEv2. Before connecting, you may need to forward port(s) on your router to the Raspberry Pi's local IP. Refer to the default port(s) for each VPN type in the next sections.

Example: Create a server on DigitalOcean

17

1. Sign up for a DigitalOcean account: Go to the DigitalOcean website (https://www.digitalocean.com) and sign up for an account if you haven't already.

2. Once you're logged in to the DigitalOcean dashboard, click the "Create" button in the top right corner of the screen and select "Droplets" from the dropdown menu.

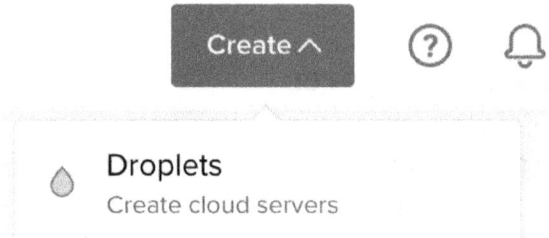

3. Select a datacenter region based on your requirements, e.g. closest to your location.

Choose Region

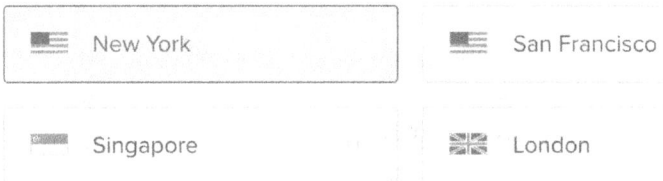

Datacenter

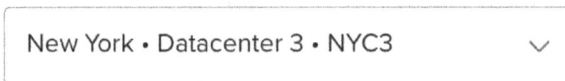

4. Under "Choose an image", select the latest Ubuntu Linux LTS version (e.g. Ubuntu 24.04) from the list of available images.

| Ubuntu | Fedora | Debian | CentOS |

Version

24.04 (LTS) x64 ⌄

5. Choose a plan for your server. You can select from various options based on your needs. For a personal VPN, a basic shared CPU plan with regular SSD disk and 1 GB memory is likely sufficient.

Droplet Type

SHARED CPU

Basic
(Plan selected)

General Purpose   CPU-Opti

CPU options

⊙ Regular
   Disk type: SSD

Premium Intel
Disk: NVMe SSD

$6/mo	$12/mo	$18/mo
$0.009/hour	$0.018/hour	$0.027/hour
←		
1 GB / 1 CPU	2 GB / 1 CPU	2 GB / 2 CPUs
25 GB SSD Disk	50 GB SSD Disk	60 GB SSD Disk
1000 GB transfer	2 TB transfer	3 TB transfer

6. Select "Password" as the authentication method, then enter a strong and secure root password. For your server's security, it is crucial that you choose a strong and secure

root password. Alternatively, you may use SSH keys for authentication.

7. Select any additional options such as backups and IPv6 if you want.

8. Enter a hostname for your server and click "Create Droplet".

9. Wait a few minutes for the server to be created.

Once your server is ready, you can connect via SSH using the username `root` and the password you entered when creating the server.

3.4.2 Connect to the server using SSH

Once your cloud server is created, you can access it via SSH. You can use the terminal on your local computer or a tool like Git for Windows to connect to your server using its IP address and your root login credentials.

To connect to your server using SSH from Windows, macOS or Linux, follow the steps below:

1. Open the terminal on your computer. On Windows, you can use a terminal emulator like Git for Windows.

   Git for Windows: https://git-scm.com/downloads
   Download the portable version, then double-click to install. When finished, open the `PortableGit` folder and double-click to run `git-bash.exe`.

2. Type the following command, replacing `username` with your username (e.g. `root`) and `server-ip` with your server's IP address or hostname:

   `ssh username@server-ip`

3. If this is your first time connecting to the server, you may be prompted to accept the server's SSH key fingerprint. Type "yes" and press enter to continue.

4. If you are using a password to log in, you will be prompted to enter your password. Type your password and press enter.

5. If this is your first time connecting to the server, and you are prompted to change the root password, enter a strong and secure new password. Otherwise, skip this step. For your server's security, it is crucial that you choose a strong and secure root password.

6. Once you are authenticated, you will be logged in to the server via SSH. You can now run commands on the server through the terminal.

7. To disconnect from the server, simply type the exit command and press enter.

3.4.3 Update the server

After connecting to the server using SSH, you can update it by running the following commands and reboot. This is optional, but recommended.

```
sudo apt update && sudo apt -y upgrade
sudo reboot
```

Linux server security best practices recommend that you regularly update your server's operating system to keep it up to date with the latest security patches and updates.

3.4.4 Install WireGuard

GitHub: https://github.com/hwdsl2/wireguard-install

First, connect to your server using SSH.

Download the WireGuard install script:

```
wget https://get.vpnsetup.net/wg -O wg.sh
```

Option 1: Auto install WireGuard using default options.

```
sudo bash wg.sh --auto
```

For servers with an external firewall (e.g. Amazon EC2), open UDP port 51820 for the VPN.

Example output:

```
$ sudo bash wg.sh --auto

WireGuard Script
https://github.com/hwdsl2/wireguard-install

Starting WireGuard setup using default options.

Server IP: 192.0.2.1
Port: UDP/51820
Client name: client
Client DNS: Google Public DNS

Installing WireGuard, please wait...
+ apt-get -yqq update
+ apt-get -yqq install wireguard qrencode
+ systemctl enable --now wg-iptables.service
+ systemctl enable --now wg-quick@wg0.service

 ---------------------------------
| QR code for client configuration |
 ---------------------------------
↑ That   is   a   QR   code   containing   the   client
configuration.

Finished!
```

The client configuration is available in: /root/client.conf
New clients can be added by running this script again.

After setup, you can run the script again to manage users or uninstall WireGuard.

Next steps: Get your computer or device to use the VPN. See:

3.5 Setting up WireGuard clients

Enjoy your very own VPN!

Option 2: Interactive install using custom options.

```
sudo bash wg.sh
```

You can customize the following options: VPN server's DNS name, UDP port, DNS server for VPN clients and name of the first client.

Example steps (replace with your own values):

Note: These options may change in newer versions of the script. Read carefully before selecting your desired option.

```
$ sudo bash wg.sh


Welcome to this WireGuard server installer!
GitHub: https://github.com/hwdsl2/wireguard-install


I need to ask you a few questions before starting
setup. You can use the default options and just press
enter if you are OK with them.
```

Enter VPN server's DNS name:

Do you want WireGuard VPN clients to connect to this server using a DNS name, e.g. vpn.example.com, instead of its IP address? [y/N] y

Enter the DNS name of this VPN server:
vpn.example.com

Select a UDP port for WireGuard:

Which port should WireGuard listen to?
Port [51820]:

Provide a name for the first client:

Enter a name for the first client:
Name [client]:

Select DNS server(s):

Select a DNS server for the client:
    1) Current system resolvers
    2) Google Public DNS
    3) Cloudflare DNS
    4) OpenDNS
    5) Quad9
    6) AdGuard DNS
    7) Custom
DNS server [2]:

Confirm and start WireGuard installation:

WireGuard installation is ready to begin.
Do you want to continue? [Y/n]

Advanced users can also auto install WireGuard using custom options. For more details, run:

```
sudo bash wg.sh -h
```

After setup, you can run the script again to manage users or uninstall WireGuard.

Next steps: Get your computer or device to use the VPN. See:

3.5 Setting up WireGuard clients

Enjoy your very own VPN!

3.4.5 Install OpenVPN

GitHub: https://github.com/hwdsl2/openvpn-install

First, connect to your server using SSH.

Download the OpenVPN install script:

```
wget https://get.vpnsetup.net/ovpn -O ovpn.sh
```

Option 1: Auto install OpenVPN using default options.

```
sudo bash ovpn.sh --auto
```

For servers with an external firewall (e.g. Amazon EC2), open UDP port 1194 for the VPN.

Example output:

```
$ sudo bash ovpn.sh --auto

OpenVPN Script
https://github.com/hwdsl2/openvpn-install

Starting OpenVPN setup using default options.
```

```
Server IP: 192.0.2.1
Port: UDP/1194
Client name: client
Client DNS: Google Public DNS

Installing OpenVPN, please wait...
+ apt-get -yqq update
+ apt-get -yqq --no-install-recommends install \
  openvpn
+ apt-get -yqq install openssl ca-certificates
+ ./easyrsa --batch init-pki
+ ./easyrsa --batch build-ca nopass
+ ./easyrsa --batch --days=3650 build-server-full \
  server nopass
+ ./easyrsa --batch --days=3650 build-client-full \
  client nopass
+ ./easyrsa --batch --days=3650 gen-crl
+ openvpn --genkey --secret \
  /etc/openvpn/server/tc.key
+ systemctl enable --now openvpn-iptables.service
+ systemctl enable --now \
  openvpn-server@server.service

Finished!


The client configuration is available in:
/root/client.ovpn
New clients can be added by running this script
again.
```

After setup, you can run the script again to manage users or uninstall OpenVPN.

Next steps: Get your computer or device to use the VPN. See:

3.6 Setting up OpenVPN clients

Enjoy your very own VPN!

Option 2: Interactive install using custom options.

```
sudo bash ovpn.sh
```

You can customize the following options: VPN server's DNS name, protocol (TCP/UDP) and port, DNS server for VPN clients and name of the first client.

Example steps (replace with your own values):

Note: These options may change in newer versions of the script. Read carefully before selecting your desired option.

```
$ sudo bash ovpn.sh

Welcome to this OpenVPN server installer!
GitHub: https://github.com/hwdsl2/openvpn-install

I need to ask you a few questions before starting
setup. You can use the default options and just press
enter if you are OK with them.
```

Enter VPN server's DNS name:

```
Do you want OpenVPN clients to connect to this server
using a DNS name, e.g. vpn.example.com, instead of
its IP address? [y/N] y

Enter the DNS name of this VPN server:
vpn.example.com
```

Select protocol and port for OpenVPN:

Which protocol should OpenVPN use?
    1) UDP (recommended)
    2) TCP
Protocol [1]:

Which port should OpenVPN listen to?
Port [1194]:

Select DNS server(s):

Select a DNS server for the clients:
    1) Current system resolvers
    2) Google Public DNS
    3) Cloudflare DNS
    4) OpenDNS
    5) Quad9
    6) AdGuard DNS
    7) Custom
DNS server [2]:

Provide a name for the first client:

Enter a name for the first client:
Name [client]:

Confirm and start OpenVPN installation:

OpenVPN installation is ready to begin.
Do you want to continue? [Y/n]

Advanced users can also auto install OpenVPN using custom options. For more details, run:

```
sudo bash ovpn.sh -h
```

After setup, you can run the script again to manage users or uninstall OpenVPN.

Next steps: Get your computer or device to use the VPN. See:

3.6 Setting up OpenVPN clients

Enjoy your very own VPN!

3.4.6 Install IPsec VPN with IKEv2

GitHub: https://github.com/hwdsl2/setup-ipsec-vpn

First, connect to your server using SSH.

Download the IPsec VPN install script:

```
wget https://get.vpnsetup.net -O vpn.sh
```

Option 1: Auto install using default options.

```
sudo sh vpn.sh
```

For servers with an external firewall (e.g. Amazon EC2), open UDP ports 500 and 4500 for the VPN.

Example output:

```
$ sudo sh vpn.sh

... ... (output omitted)
===================================

IPsec VPN server is now ready for use!

Connect to your new VPN with these details:
```

```
Server IP: 192.0.2.1
IPsec PSK: [Your IPsec PSK]
Username: vpnuser
Password: [Your VPN Password]
```

Write these down. You'll need them to connect!

VPN client setup: https://vpnsetup.net/clients

```
==================================

==================================
```

IKEv2 setup successful. Details for IKEv2 mode:

VPN server address: 192.0.2.1
VPN client name: vpnclient

Client configuration is available at:
/root/vpnclient.p12 (for Windows & Linux)
/root/vpnclient.sswan (for Android)
/root/vpnclient.mobileconfig (for iOS & macOS)

Next steps: Configure IKEv2 clients. See:
https://vpnsetup.net/clients

```
==================================
```

After setup, you can run sudo ikev2.sh to manage IKEv2 clients.

Next steps: Get your computer or device to use the VPN. See:

Configure IKEv2 VPN clients:
https://github.com/hwdsl2/setup-ipsec-vpn#next-steps

Enjoy your very own VPN!

Option 2: Interactive install using custom options.

```
sudo VPN_SKIP_IKEV2=yes sh vpn.sh
sudo ikev2.sh
```

You can customize the following options: VPN server's DNS name, name and validity period of the first client, DNS server for VPN clients and whether to password protect client config files.

Example steps (replace with your own values):

Note: These options may change in newer versions of the script. Read carefully before selecting your desired option.

```
$ sudo VPN_SKIP_IKEV2=yes sh vpn.sh
... ... (output omitted)

$ sudo ikev2.sh


Welcome! Use this script to set up IKEv2 on your VPN
server.

I need to ask you a few questions before starting
setup. You can use the default options and just press
enter if you are OK with them.
```

Enter VPN server's DNS name:

```
Do you want IKEv2 clients to connect to this server
using a DNS name, e.g. vpn.example.com, instead of
```

```
its IP address? [y/N] y


Enter the DNS name of this VPN server:
vpn.example.com
```

Enter name and validity period for the first client:

```
Provide a name for the IKEv2 client.
Use one word only, no special characters except '-'
and '_'.
Client name: [vpnclient]

Specify the validity period (in months) for this
client certificate.
Enter an integer between 1 and 120: [120]
```

Specify custom DNS server(s):

```
By default, clients are set to use Google Public DNS
when the VPN is active.
Do you want to specify custom DNS servers for IKEv2?
[y/N] y


Enter primary DNS server: 1.1.1.1
Enter secondary DNS server (Enter to skip): 1.0.0.1
```

Select whether to password protect client config files:

```
IKEv2 client config files contain the client
certificate, private key and CA certificate. This
script can optionally generate a random password to
protect these files.


Protect client config files using a password? [y/N]
```

Review and confirm setup options:

```
We are ready to set up IKEv2 now.
Below are the setup options you selected.


======================================


Server address: vpn.example.com
Client name: vpnclient

Client cert valid for: 120 months
MOBIKE support: Not available
Protect client config: No
DNS server(s): 1.1.1.1 1.0.0.1


======================================


Do you want to continue? [Y/n]
```

After setup, you can run sudo ikev2.sh to manage IKEv2 clients.

Next steps: Get your computer or device to use the VPN. See:

Configure IKEv2 VPN clients:
https://github.com/hwdsl2/setup-ipsec-vpn#next-steps

Enjoy your very own VPN!

3.4.7 Transfer files from the server

When configuring VPN clients, you may need to securely transfer client configuration file(s) from the server to your local computer. One way to do this is by using the scp command. Example steps:

1. Open the terminal on your computer. On Windows, you can use a terminal emulator like Git for Windows.

   Git for Windows: https://git-scm.com/downloads
   Download the portable version, then double-click to install. When finished, open the `PortableGit` folder and double-click to run `git-bash.exe`.

2. Type the following command, replacing `username` with your SSH username (e.g. `root`), `server-ip` with your server's IP address or hostname, `/path/to/file` with the path to the file on the server, and `/local/folder` with the local folder where you want to save the file.

```
scp username@server-ip:/path/to/file /local/folder
```

3. For example, if you want to authenticate as `root` and transfer `/root/client.conf` from the server with IP address `192.0.2.1` to the current working folder on the local computer:

```
scp root@192.0.2.1:/root/client.conf ./
```

   Note: If using Git for Windows, the local folder / usually points to the installation folder, e.g. `PortableGit`.

4. If you are using a password to log in, you will be prompted to enter your password. Type your password and press enter.

5. The file will then be transferred from the server and saved to the local folder you specified.

3.4.8 Uninstall the VPN

If you want to remove WireGuard, OpenVPN and/or IPsec VPN from the server, follow these steps.

Warning: All VPN configuration will be **permanently deleted**. This **cannot be undone**!

First, connect to your server using SSH.

To uninstall WireGuard, run:

```
sudo bash wg.sh
```

You will see the following options:

```
WireGuard is already installed.
```

```
Select an option:
  1) Add a new client
  2) List existing clients
  3) Remove an existing client
  4) Show QR code for a client
  5) Remove WireGuard
  6) Exit
```

Select option 5 from the menu, by typing 5 and pressing enter. Then confirm the WireGuard removal.

Note: These options may change in newer versions of the script. Read carefully before selecting your desired option.

To uninstall OpenVPN, run:

```
sudo bash ovpn.sh
```

You will see the following options:

```
OpenVPN is already installed.

Select an option:
 1) Add a new client
 2) Export config for an existing client
 3) List existing clients
 4) Revoke an existing client
 5) Remove OpenVPN
 6) Exit
```

Select option 5 from the menu, by typing 5 and pressing enter. Then confirm the OpenVPN removal.

To uninstall IPsec VPN, download and run the helper script:

```
wget https://get.vpnsetup.net/unst -O unst.sh
sudo bash unst.sh
```

When prompted, confirm the IPsec VPN removal.

3.5 Setting up WireGuard clients

WireGuard VPN clients are available for Windows, macOS, iOS, Android and Linux:
https://www.wireguard.com/install/

To add a VPN connection, open the WireGuard app on your mobile device, tap the "Add" button, then scan the QR code or import the .conf configuration file from your VPN provider or your own server. For Windows and macOS, first securely transfer the .conf file to your computer, then open WireGuard and import the file.

To manage WireGuard VPN users on your own server, run the install script again: `sudo bash wg.sh`.

3.5.1 Windows

1. Securely transfer the `.conf` file to your computer.
2. Install and launch the WireGuard VPN client (https://www.wireguard.com/install/).
3. Click **Import tunnel(s) from file**.
4. Browse to and select the `.conf` file, then click **Open**.
5. Click **Activate**.

3.5.2 macOS

1. Securely transfer the `.conf` file to your computer.
2. Install and launch the **WireGuard** app from **App Store**.
3. Click **Import tunnel(s) from file**.
4. Browse to and select the `.conf` file, then click **Open**.
5. Click **Activate**.

3.5.3 Android

1. Install and launch the **WireGuard** app from **Google Play**.
2. Tap the "+" button, then tap **Scan from QR code**.
3. Scan the QR code from your VPN server.
4. Enter anything you like for the **Tunnel Name**.
5. Tap **Create tunnel**.
6. Slide the switch ON for the new VPN profile.

3.5.4 iOS (iPhone/iPad)

1. Install and launch the **WireGuard** app from **App Store**.
2. Tap **Add a tunnel**, then tap **Create from QR code**.
3. Scan the QR code from your VPN server.
4. Enter anything you like for the tunnel name.

5. Tap **Save**.

6. Slide the switch ON for the new VPN profile.

3.5.5 Linux

Install the package and tools:

```
sudo apt update
sudo apt install wireguard -y
```

Your VPN provider or your server gives you a .conf configuration file or individual keys. A basic /etc/wireguard/wg0.conf looks like:

```
[Interface]
PrivateKey = <your_private_key>
Address = 10.0.0.2/24

[Peer]
PublicKey = <server_public_key>
Endpoint = vpn.example.com:51820
AllowedIPs = 0.0.0.0/0
PersistentKeepalive = 25
```

Note: The AllowedIPs = 0.0.0.0/0 means all traffic goes through the VPN (default gateway). You can customize that (split tunneling) by using a more specific subnet for AllowedIPs.

Save the configuration as /etc/wireguard/wg0.conf (with proper ownership: chmod 600 wg0.conf). Then start WireGuard:

```
sudo wg-quick up wg0
```

This creates the `wg0` interface and routes traffic through it. To make it start at boot:

```
sudo systemctl enable wg-quick@wg0
```

Verify status with `wg show wg0` to ensure it's connected. WireGuard's simplicity means **no additional tunneling software** is needed beyond the kernel module and `wg-quick`.

3.6 Setting up OpenVPN clients

OpenVPN clients (https://openvpn.net/client/) are available for Windows, macOS, iOS, Android and Linux. macOS users can also use Tunnelblick (https://tunnelblick.net).

To add a VPN connection, first securely transfer the `.ovpn` file from your VPN provider or your own server to your device, then open the OpenVPN app and import the VPN profile.

To manage OpenVPN users on your own server, run the install script again: `sudo bash ovpn.sh`.

3.6.1 Windows

1. Securely transfer the `.ovpn` file to your computer.
2. Download and install OpenVPN Connect (https://openvpn.net/client/).
3. Launch the **OpenVPN Connect** VPN client.
4. On the **Get connected** screen, click the **Upload file** tab.
5. Drag and drop the `.ovpn` file into the window, or browse to and select the `.ovpn` file, then click **Open**.
6. Click **Connect**.

3.6.2 macOS

1. Securely transfer the .ovpn file to your computer.
2. Install and launch Tunnelblick (https://tunnelblick.net).
3. On the welcome screen, click **I have configuration files**.
4. On the **Add a Configuration** screen, click **OK**.
5. Click the Tunnelblick icon in the menu bar, then select **VPN Details**.
6. Drag and drop the .ovpn file into the **Configurations** window (left pane).
7. Follow on-screen instructions to install the OpenVPN profile.
8. Click **Connect**.

3.6.3 Android

1. Securely transfer the .ovpn file to your Android device.
2. Install and launch **OpenVPN Connect** from **Google Play**.
3. On the **Get connected** screen, tap the **Upload file** tab.
4. Tap **Browse**, then browse to and select the .ovpn file.
   Note: To find the .ovpn file, tap the three-line menu button, then browse to the location you saved the file.
5. On the **Imported Profile** screen, tap **Connect**.

3.6.4 iOS (iPhone/iPad)

First, install and launch **OpenVPN Connect** from **App Store**. Then securely transfer the .ovpn file to your iOS device. To transfer the file, you may use:

1. AirDrop the file and open with OpenVPN, or

2. Upload to your device (OpenVPN app folder) using File Sharing (https://support.apple.com/en-us/119585), then launch the OpenVPN Connect app and tap the **File** tab.

When finished, tap **Add** to import the VPN profile, then tap **Connect**.

To customize settings for the OpenVPN Connect App, tap the three-line menu button, then tap **Settings**.

3.6.5 Linux

Install the package and tools:

```
sudo apt update
sudo apt install openvpn -y
```

Assuming that you have an .ovpn configuration file from your VPN provider or your own server, you can connect with:

```
sudo openvpn --config /path/to/client.ovpn
```

This will run OpenVPN in the terminal. You'll see log outputs as it connects. To run OpenVPN client as a background service, refer to the OpenVPN wiki: https://community.openvpn.net/Pages/Systemd

3.7 VPN kill switch and leak protection

A key feature is a *kill switch* (or *network lock*): If the VPN connection drops, the kill switch cuts all traffic to prevent leaks. Many VPN clients have an option (often under "Settings → Firewall / Kill Switch") to enable this. For example, in WireGuard on Windows, there is an "Always-on VPN" option;

on Android, you can enable a block for "when VPN not connected". On Linux, you can write firewall rules. Example (with `iptables` on Debian/Ubuntu):

```
# Only allow traffic via wg0,
# block eth0 (or wlan0) if wg0 is down
sudo iptables -A OUTPUT ! -o wg0 -m conntrack \
  --ctstate NEW,ESTABLISHED -j DROP
```

This line says: Any new or existing outbound connection not on the wg0 interface should be dropped. (Be careful: Test in a console before rebooting, to avoid locking yourself out.) The exact rules depend on your distro's firewall (ufw, firewalld, etc.). Many distributions have **ufw** (Uncomplicated Firewall); you can do something like:

```
sudo ufw default deny outgoing
sudo ufw allow out on wg0
sudo ufw allow in on wg0
sudo ufw enable
```

This blocks all outgoing traffic unless it's on the VPN. (The above is a simplified example, adjust it to your needs.) Graphical clients often have this built-in, but understanding the underlying firewall rules is useful for servers/routers.

4 Secure DNS and Local Resolvers

Even with a VPN, your device still performs DNS lookups. If the VPN doesn't configure DNS, your system may default to the ISP's DNS (which might log your queries). To plug this gap, use encrypted DNS or a local resolver.

4.1 Why DNS privacy matters

DNS (Domain Name System) translates names to IPs. In unprotected form, **every device on your network is shouting "What is the IP of example.com?" in plaintext**. The response goes back similarly. Eavesdroppers (including your ISP or Wi-Fi hotspot operator) can log every site you visit via these queries. Even with a VPN, if the VPN has a misconfiguration or you use split tunneling, DNS might still leak.

Tools to protect DNS privacy:

- **DNS over HTTPS (DoH)**: Encrypts DNS queries using HTTPS. Browsers like Firefox and Chrome support DoH, and OSes (Windows 11, Android 9+) support it.

- **DNS over TLS (DoT)**: Encrypts DNS queries over TLS (port 853 by default). Android's "Private DNS" is DoT.

- **Encrypted DNSCrypt**: An older but still-used protocol (DNSCrypt) that encrypts DNS between client and server. The dnscrypt-proxy tool can serve as a client and forward queries to encrypted DNS servers.

- **DNSSEC**: Cryptographically signs DNS records. It ensures integrity (no tampering), but does not encrypt the queries themselves. It's often used together with above.

Local recursive resolver (Unbound): Instead of using a third-party resolver, you can run your own DNS resolver on your device or router. This way, your device queries *your local Unbound server* (often at 127.0.0.1), and Unbound recursively fetches the answer from the root/authoritative servers. If Unbound is misconfigured (no encryption), your ISP could still see those queries (unless you pair it with upstream DoT/DoH). But the advantage: You can apply filtering (block ads/malware) and avoid relying on third-party logs. Red Hat notes that "by using your own resolver you stop sharing your DNS traffic with third parties and increase your DNS privacy".

4.2 Encrypted DNS examples

Windows 11 (DNS over HTTPS): Windows 11 has built-in DoH support. In Settings → Network & Internet → Wireless (or Ethernet) → [your adapter] → DNS server assignment, you can set DNS and choose "Encrypted only (DNS over HTTPS)". If your DNS provider (like Cloudflare, Quad9) is pre-configured, select it. If not, you can add a custom DoH server.

macOS: Newer macOS (Big Sur and later) natively support DNS over TLS (DoT) and DNS over HTTPS (DoH) via configuration profiles. Please refer to the setup guide from your DNS provider, e.g. Quad9 (https://docs.quad9.net).

Android: On Android 9 and newer, go to **Settings →
Network & Internet → Advanced → Private DNS**. Enter
a DNS provider hostname (e.g. `dns.google` for Google,
`dns.quad9.net` for Quad9, `1dot1dot1dot1.cloudflare-
dns.com` for Cloudflare) and save. This enables DoT for all
apps.

iOS: In iOS 14+, Apple introduced "iCloud Private Relay" for
Safari (covered later). For DNS, iPhones use the DNS of the
connected Wi-Fi or cellular by default. You can use VPN
profiles or apps (like AdGuard DNS app) to set DNS to
encrypted servers. There is no built-in system UI for DoT on
iOS.

Linux: Tools like `systemd-resolved` support DoH/DoT, or
you may use `dnscrypt-proxy` or `cloudflared`. For example, to
use Cloudflare's DoT with `systemd-resolved`, add to
`/etc/systemd/resolved.conf`:

```
[Resolve]
DNS=1.1.1.1
FallbackDNS=1.0.0.1
DNSOverTLS=yes
```

Then run `sudo systemctl restart systemd-resolved`. Now
`/etc/resolv.conf` points to 127.0.0.53 which is systemd-
resolved, but queries go encrypted to Cloudflare.

4.3 DNS provider comparison

Below is a comparison of popular public DNS providers with a
privacy focus, summarizing their features:

DNS Service	IPv4 Addresses	Privacy & Features Summary
Cloudflare	1.1.1.1, 1.0.0.1	Supports DoH/DoT. Fast global network, optional malware/adult content blocking (1.1.1.2/1.1.1.3).
Quad9	9.9.9.9, 149.112.112.112	Blocks known malicious domains. Supports DoH/DoT/DNSCrypt.
Google Public DNS	8.8.8.8, 8.8.4.4	Supports DoH. Reliable and fast.
AdGuard DNS	94.140.14.14, 94.140.15.15	Ad-blocking (also safe search modes). Supports DoH/DoT/DNSCrypt. Offers filtering (ads/malware).
NextDNS	Varies	User-configurable logging, query minimization. Extensive filtering available (ads, trackers, threats).
Mullvad DNS	193.138.219.74, 193.138.218.74	Offers content/ad blocking. Great privacy, though smaller scale.
OpenDNS (Cisco)	208.67.222.222, 208.67.220.220	Business oriented; filters and parental controls available.
ControlD	Varies	Supports filters, DoH/DoT/DoQ.

DNS Provider Notes: Cloudflare and Quad9 are often recommended for privacy-conscious users. Cloudflare's policy of deleting logs quickly is strong, but note its US jurisdiction. Quad9's strict no-IP-logs policy and Swiss location are appealing. AdGuard is unique for built-in ad blocking, useful for families or those wanting to reduce tracking. NextDNS is highly customizable and privacy-respecting, but requires a bit more setup (using their iOS/Android app, or manual DNS entries).

4.4 Unbound as a local resolver

Running **Unbound** provides additional control. On Linux/FreeBSD, Unbound can serve as a caching, recursive DNS resolver that you point your system's DNS to (127.0.0.1 by default). Benefits include DNSSEC validation, caching for speed, and ability to apply Response Policy Zones (RPZ) to block domains (e.g. ads, trackers). However, by default, Unbound will query root servers in plaintext. To encrypt those queries, you can:

- Configure forwarders in Unbound to use DoT/DoH upstream (e.g. Cloudflare or Quad9 over TLS).
- Use the `stub` directive (e.g. `stub-zone:`) for encrypted servers.

Installation example (Ubuntu):

```
sudo apt update
sudo apt install unbound -y
```

Basic config example:

Edit `/etc/unbound/unbound.conf` (or create a file in `/etc/unbound/conf.d/`):

```
server:
  interface: 127.0.0.1
  access-control: 127.0.0.1 allow
  root-hints: "/etc/unbound/root.hints"
  auto-trust-anchor-file: "/var/lib/unbound/root.key"

forward-zone:
  name: "."
  forward-addr: 1.1.1.1@853   # Cloudflare DoT
  forward-addr: 1.0.0.1@853   # Cloudflare secondary
  # Alternatively, for Quad9:
  # forward-addr: 9.9.9.9@853
```

This tells Unbound to listen on localhost and forward everything via encrypted Cloudflare. You'd need to fetch up-to-date root.hints (`wget -O /etc/unbound/root.hints https://www.internic.net/domain/named.root`) and run `unbound-anchor` to get root.key for DNSSEC. Then start Unbound: `sudo systemctl enable unbound && sudo systemctl start unbound`.

Test it:

```
dig example.com @127.0.0.1
```

Look for `SERVER: 127.0.0.1#53` in the dig output. If it shows `127.0.0.1#53`, Unbound answered. Compare `dig example.com` (with default resolver) shows `SERVER: 127.0.0.53#53` on Ubuntu, indicating systemd-resolved is answering.

Note on privacy: As Red Hat notes, using your own Unbound means you're not sharing DNS with Google/Cloudflare by default. However, to shield from your

49

ISP, ensure you use DNS encryption for the upstream. You could also run Unbound on your router (if supported) to serve your home network.

4.5 Dnscrypt-proxy and other tools

The tool `dnscrypt-proxy` is another way to encrypt DNS. It can act as a local DNS server, forwarding to chosen DNSCrypt or DoH providers.

Installation on Linux (e.g. Ubuntu):

```
sudo apt install dnscrypt-proxy
```

It installs to `/etc/dnscrypt-proxy/dnscrypt-proxy.toml`. Edit that file to select servers (like `'cloudflare'`, `'quad9-dnscrypt-ip4'`) and set `listen_addresses = ['127.0.0.1:53']`. Then:

```
sudo systemctl enable dnscrypt-proxy
sudo systemctl start dnscrypt-proxy
```

Now point your system DNS to 127.0.0.1. `dnscrypt-proxy` will encrypt queries (to e.g. Cloudflare's DNSCrypt endpoint).

While we won't cover every variation, the key idea is: **encrypt your DNS**. Whether via OS settings, browser (Firefox's DNS-over-HTTPS setting), or local proxies like `dnscrypt-proxy`, you prevent on-path observers from knowing your DNS queries. This greatly improves privacy, as even your ISP cannot tell which sites you are looking up.

5 Browser and Online Privacy Tools

After securing the network layer, we must harden the endpoint: the web browser or app through which you spend the most time. Modern browsers have built-in privacy features and support extensions. Here we cover general strategies and specific browser tools.

5.1 Tracking prevention and ad blocking

Most browsers now include features to block cross-site trackers and fingerprinting. For example, **Safari** uses Intelligent Tracking Prevention (ITP) by default. It hides your IP from trackers and blocks known third-party cookies. In Private Browsing mode, Safari goes further: "Known trackers are completely prevented from loading on pages, and link tracking protection removes tracking added to URLs as you browse".

Firefox offers **Enhanced Tracking Protection**, blocking known trackers and cryptominers by default (usually "Standard" mode blocks social trackers, "Strict" blocks more). Its **Facebook Container** and **Multi-Account Containers** (extensions) let you isolate sites into separate containers, preventing cookie-based cross-site tracking.

Ad blockers: Extensions like uBlock Origin (browser plugin or system-wide) can block ads, trackers, and even scripts. Blocking ads is not just about speed/cleanliness; it also prevents many tracking scripts from loading at all. For example, you might use **uBlock Origin** on Chrome/Firefox, or use **Brave** browser which has built-in strong ad and tracker blocking.

Fingerprinting protection: Some browsers (Firefox, Brave, Safari) try to reduce fingerprintability. Safari "presents a simplified system configuration so more devices look identical to trackers". Brave and Firefox can block or randomize some identifiers (e.g. canvas fingerprint blocking in Brave Shields, Resist Fingerprinting in Firefox's privacy options).

5.2 Private browsing and containers

Use private/incognito mode for sessions you don't want to be saved. This prevents local history and cookies from persisting. However, note: private mode does *not* hide your traffic from network observers (it's still as exposed as normal mode). It mainly helps on the same device.

For longer-term separation, browser **containers** (Firefox's Multi-Account Container extension, for example) are great. You can assign identities (containers) to different sites (e.g. work vs personal). Each container has its own storage, so cookies in one don't leak to others. This stops, for example, Facebook tracking your visits on other sites via shared cookies. Example usage: Gmail in one container, banks in another, social media in a third container.

5.3 Browser privacy comparison

A quick outline of popular browsers and their privacy features:

- **Safari (Apple):** Intelligent Tracking Prevention (ITP) by default; Privacy Reports; sandboxing. Private Browsing auto-locks windows when idle (requires authentication). Apple's stance is strong on privacy (also built-in VPN-like Private Relay, see Chapter 7).

- **Firefox (Mozilla):** Strong default tracking protection; open-source; supports extensive privacy extensions. Social and cross-site trackers blocked by default. Users can tweak "Strict" mode for more blocking.

- **Brave:** Built-in ad & tracker blocking (Brave Shields), fingerprint randomization, integrated Tor windows (built on Chromium). Privacy-first by design; also has a built-in Brave Firewall+VPN on some platforms.

- **DuckDuckGo Privacy Browser (mobile):** Focuses on privacy; blocks trackers; uses DuckDuckGo search by default; simpler UI.

- **Google Chrome and Microsoft Edge:** By default, more permissive; but both have incognito mode and optional DoH. Extensions needed for more privacy (like uBlock Origin, HTTPS Everywhere). Edge (Chromium) has some tracking prevention levels.

- **Tor Browser:** Most private (based on Firefox ESR). Routes traffic through Tor network (multiple hops). Protects against network surveillance and fingerprinting by design (all users appear identical). Main drawback is speed and some site incompatibilities.

We cannot list every browser, but as a rule: Use a browser that lets you block trackers easily and updates frequently. For day-to-day, Firefox or Brave are good; use Tor Browser for high anonymity needs (e.g. circumventing censorship).

5.4 Secure browser configurations

Below are some tips on secure browser configurations, regardless of browser choice:

- Use HTTPS everywhere. Many browsers default to HTTPS now or have "HTTPS-Only" mode (Firefox). The **HTTPS Everywhere** extension (by EFF) can force HTTPS where available.

- Disable WebRTC leak. Browsers with WebRTC (Chrome, Firefox, Edge) can leak your real IP in certain conditions. Extensions or settings to disable WebRTC (e.g. in Firefox `media.peerconnection.enabled` = `false` in `about:config`) help prevent that leak.

- Enable "Do Not Track" (although most trackers ignore it). More importantly, use uBlock Origin or built-in content blockers.

- Avoid installing many extensions (each is additional attack surface). Stick to well-known ones and keep them updated.

- Disable Autofill/Password saving in the browser if using a dedicated password manager (for security hygiene).

5.5 Example: Enabling Firefox's DoH

As a practical step-by-step, here's how to enable DNS-over-HTTPS in Firefox (cross-platform):

1. Open **Settings** → **General** → **Network Settings** (bottom of page).
2. Click **Settings...** next to "Network Settings."
3. Scroll down and check **Enable DNS over HTTPS**.
4. Choose a provider (Cloudflare by default) or enter a custom one.
5. Click **OK**.

Now Firefox will send DNS through HTTPS, regardless of system DNS. You can verify it in about:networking#dns (Firefox 98+) or about:debugging#/runtime/this-firefox in older versions.

6 Operating System and Device Privacy Settings

Beyond apps and networks, your device OS has built-in privacy controls. We cover key settings on Windows, macOS, Android, and iOS, as well as certain browser extensions and system-wide tools.

6.1 Windows privacy

Windows 11/10 Settings:

- **Privacy & security settings:** Go to **Settings → Privacy & security** to configure security settings and Windows/App permissions. For example, under **Windows permissions → General**, you can disable toggles like "Let apps show me personalized ads by using my advertising ID".

- **Permissions:** Under **Privacy & security → App permissions**, control which apps can access camera, microphone, location, etc. Only allow essential apps to use these.

- **Location Services:** Turn off location if not needed, or limit to certain apps.

- **Diagnostics and Telemetry:** In **Settings → Privacy & security → Diagnostics & feedback**, set Diagnostic data to "Required" only, and turn off tailored experiences. (Enterprise management may allow more control via group policy).

- **Limit data sharing with Microsoft:** Turn off sending additional Microsoft product usage data.

- **Windows Firewall & VPN:** Ensure the built-in firewall is on. A built-in Windows VPN (SSTP, PPTP, IKEv2) can also be configured under **Network & Internet → VPN** if not using third-party clients.

- **BitLocker:** Enable BitLocker full-disk encryption to protect data on your computer (Settings → Privacy & security → Device encryption).

6.2 macOS privacy

macOS has a strong security model. Key steps:

- **System Preferences → Security & Privacy:** Under Privacy tab, review **Location Services, Contacts, Calendars, Camera, Microphone, Full Disk Access, Screen Recording**, etc. Only grant apps exactly what they need.

- **Safari Security:** Safari's preferences include enabling Fraudulent Website Warning, blocking pop-ups/ads, and others.

- **FileVault:** Enable FileVault (full disk encryption) to protect data at rest.

- **Gatekeeper & Updates:** Keep macOS updated. In Security & Privacy → General, allow only App Store or App Store + identified developers.

- **Firewall:** Turn on the macOS firewall (Security & Privacy → Firewall). The "Stealth Mode" option hides your Mac from probing.

6.3 Android privacy

Android has enhanced privacy in recent versions:

- **Permissions:** Under Settings → Privacy → Permission manager, review per-permission usage (Location, Camera, etc.). Revoke any unwanted.

- **Location Services:** You can allow location only while app is in use, or turn off at system level.

- **Background Activity:** Settings → Apps → See all → [app] → Battery, restrict background usage for apps that don't need it.

- **Private DNS:** As covered earlier in this book, set Private DNS to an encrypted resolver (Settings → Network & Internet → Advanced → Private DNS).

- **Lockscreen Notifications:** Limit what shows on lockscreen if device locked.

- **Google Services:** In Google settings (Accounts), turn off ad personalization and "Allow usage & diagnostics" to Google.

- **Android 14+:** The Privacy Dashboard shows how often apps accessed sensitive data. Use it to check unusual behavior. Also, Privacy Sandbox features (like FLoC alternatives) are emerging.

6.4 iOS privacy

iOS is known for granular controls:

- **Settings → Privacy & Security:** Check each category (Location Services, Contacts, Photos, Microphone, etc.) and turn off unwanted access.

- **Trackers:** In Settings → Privacy & Security → Tracking, disable "Allow Apps to Request to Track" to stop app tracking requests.

- **Safari:** In Settings → (Apps →) Safari, enable "Prevent Cross-Site Tracking" and "Hide IP Address" (since iOS 14). Also see "Privacy Report" to review blocked trackers.

- **App Privacy Report:** iOS 15+ can generate a report showing app sensor/network access (Settings → Privacy & Security → App Privacy Report). Enable it to audit apps.

- **Location Services:** Under Privacy & Security → Location Services, you can configure various options depending on your needs, such as permissions for apps and system services.

- **Analytics & Improvements:** Go to Privacy & Security → Analytics & Improvements to configure whether to share iPhone analytics and other options such as "Improve Siri and Dictation".

iCloud Private Relay: If you have iCloud+ (now part of Apple One etc), you can use Private Relay (Settings → [Your Name] → iCloud → Private Relay). This encrypts Safari traffic by relaying through two servers: one knows your IP, the other knows the destination, so no single party learns both. (We cover it in detail in the next chapter.)

6.5 Browser extensions and utilities

Aside from OS and device privacy settings, you can further enhance your privacy with browser extensions and system-wide tools:

- **VPN Apps:** We covered in earlier chapters. On mobile, install your VPN's app to connect and route traffic through the VPN.

- **AdGuard (App-level):** On mobile, AdGuard has apps (Android, iOS) that provide system-wide DNS filtering (using local VPN technique). They enforce encrypted DNS, block ads, and can filter trackers even outside the browser.

- **Password Manager:** While not covered in depth here, using a password manager (like Bitwarden or 1Password) can improve security. iOS and Android allow integration with system autofill. Some browsers, such as Google Chrome, has "password monitoring" features that can alert you if any of your saved passwords appears in a data leak.

- **Two-Factor Authenticator:** Use an authenticator app (Authy, Google Authenticator) instead of SMS for 2FA. This doesn't directly protect network traffic, but could be a key part of overall security hygiene.

7 Apple's iCloud Private Relay

With iOS 15/macOS Monterey, Apple introduced **iCloud Private Relay** for Safari. Understanding how it compares to traditional tools:

- **What it does:** When on Safari, after enabling iCloud Private Relay, your DNS and web traffic are encrypted and sent through *two relays* run by two different entities. The first relay (Apple-run) knows your IP but assigns a temporary random one. The second relay (partner CDN) knows the site you're visiting but sees only an obfuscated IP (Apple's). This ensures *no single party can see both you and your destination*. It hides your IP from websites (they see a relay IP) and hides your browsing content from your ISP. DNS queries are also encrypted and proxied.

- **Limitations:** Private Relay only works in Safari (and certain apps using system network stack, e.g. Weather). It does *not* handle traffic from other browsers or apps. It requires iCloud+ subscription. It also might not work with custom DNS or on certain networks unless you enable "Limit IP Address Tracking" on Wi-Fi or Cellular networks (as shown in Apple's guide). Some regional restrictions apply (not available everywhere).

- **Privacy profile:** It's somewhat like a lightweight VPN for Safari only. Because Apple mandates each relay be run by a different company, even Apple itself can't see both ends. In Apple's words, "no single party (not even Apple or your network provider) can match an IP address to a website". Websites see only a generic location (country/time zone) if you allow it.

This chapter dives deep into iCloud Private Relay: its design goals, privacy model, limitations, practical setup on iPhone/iPad and Mac, as well as troubleshooting. You'll get step-by-step configuration instructions and checks to verify whether Private Relay is active.

7.1 Overview: What is iCloud Private Relay?

Apple's iCloud Private Relay is a privacy feature for iCloud+ subscribers that aims to hide your Safari web browsing (and some system DNS lookups) from network observers. Its core idea is split trust: Traffic is routed through two separate relays so that no single party can see both who you are and which websites you visit.

Ingress relay (Apple): Sees the user's IP address but not the destination hostname (the request contents are encrypted).

Egress relay (partner CDNs): Sees the website destination but receives only a temporary, region-appropriate IP that does not identify the user.

This design means:

- Apple cannot link your real IP to your browsing destination.

- Your ISP / local network cannot read the DNS or the full destination of your Safari traffic.

- It does not provide the same coverage as a full-device VPN —Private Relay primarily protects Safari traffic.

7.2 Benefits & trade-offs

Benefits:

- Easy to enable: Built into iOS / macOS for iCloud+ users (single toggle).

- No per-app configuration: Works automatically for Safari and certain system resolver lookups.

- Split-trust model: No single network operator (not even Apple) sees both your identity and destinations.

- Encrypts Safari DNS & traffic: Protects browsing from local network snooping (e.g. public Wi-Fi).

Trade-offs / Limitations:

- Only covers Safari (and some system DNS). Traffic from other browsers or apps is not automatically relayed.

- No server-selection (cannot choose country-specific exit IPs like you can with a VPN).

- Not a drop-in replacement for a VPN or Tor when full-device coverage or maximum anonymity is required.

- Unavailable on some managed/captive networks or in certain countries / regulatory environments.

7.3 Who should use Private Relay?

iCloud Private Relay may be suitable for:

- Everyday Apple users who want a convenient, privacy-enhancing feature for web browsing.

- People who want to hide their Safari browsing from local networks and ISPs without installing third-party apps.

- Users who prefer a split-trust architecture over trusting a single VPN provider with all their traffic.

It is not ideal for:

- Users who need to route all app traffic through a third-party location (e.g. to access region-locked services via a different country).

- Users who require high anonymity against adversaries—use Tor for that.

7.4 Prerequisites and compatibility

Before configuring Private Relay:

1. You must have an iCloud+ subscription under the Apple ID you use on the device.

2. Update to a supported OS version:

   - iOS/iPadOS: recent versions (iOS 15+ features improved behavior; use the latest stable release).

   - macOS: Monterey or later (with latest patches) for best compatibility.

3. Private Relay may be unavailable on certain networks, regions, or managed devices (MDM/enterprise-managed profiles).

7.5 Enable & configure Private Relay on iPhone / iPad

1. Open Settings → tap your Apple ID (your name) → iCloud.

2. Tap Private Relay.

3. Toggle Private Relay to On.

4. Next to the toggle, you can configure IP Address Location option:

   - Maintain general location, or
   - Use country and time zone

5. Optionally, configure per-network behavior:

   - Open Settings → Wi-Fi → (tap 🛈 next to a network) → toggle Limit IP Address Tracking. This enables/disables Private Relay for that specific Wi-Fi.

Notes:

If you try to toggle Private Relay and it shows Not Available, see troubleshooting steps below.

If you have a full-device VPN active, Private Relay may be disabled or may not function as expected, to avoid overlapping tunneling technologies that conflict.

7.6 Enable & configure Private Relay on macOS

1. Open System Settings (Apple menu → System Settings) → click your Apple ID → iCloud.

2. Find Private Relay and toggle it On.

3. Set IP Address Location preferences (same options as iOS).

4. To configure per-network behavior: Open System Settings → Network → Wi-Fi → Details for network → Limit IP Address Tracking (toggle on/off).

Notes:

iCloud Private Relay affects Safari browsing on macOS. CLI tools (Terminal curl, etc.) generally do not use Private Relay; they may use the system network stack, but may not be routed via the relay in the same way Safari is.

7.7 How to verify Private Relay is active

Below are practical checks to confirm Private Relay is functioning for Safari:

Visual status in Settings (quick check)

- iPhone: Settings → Apple ID → iCloud → Private Relay shows On or Off.

- macOS: System Settings → Apple ID → iCloud → Private Relay shows status.

Use Safari and check your IP via a web service

- Open Safari and visit a public "what is my IP" site (e.g. https://ipchicken.com or http://ipv4.icanhazip.com).

- If Private Relay is on, the public IP shown should be different than your ISP-assigned IP.

Important note: Because Private Relay specifically targets Safari (and some system DNS), these tests should be performed in Safari. Using other browsers, or running `curl http://ipv4.icanhazip.com` from Terminal on macOS may show your real IP.

7.8 Troubleshooting Private Relay

If Private Relay does not appear to be working or shows Not Available:

1. Confirm iCloud+ subscription and Apple ID. Go to Settings → Apple ID → iCloud and verify you're signed into the same Apple ID and that iCloud+ is active.

2. Check OS version. Update to the latest iOS/iPadOS/macOS release to ensure compatibility.

3. Disable conflicting network tools:

   o VPN clients (full-device) often disable Private Relay—turn your VPN off temporarily to test.

   o Local DNS proxies or packet-capturing tools could interfere with Private Relay.

4. Network restrictions: Some networks (enterprise-managed, captive portals, or certain ISPs) block Private Relay. Try a different Wi-Fi or cellular network.

5. Check MDM/Profiles: Devices managed by an organization (MDM) can have settings or restrictions that prevent Private Relay.

6. Toggle Private Relay off/on: Sometimes re-authenticating the iCloud account or toggling the feature off and on can fix transient issues. You could also try restarting your device.

7.9 Advanced: Interaction with VPNs, DNS, and browsers

iCloud Private Relay vs. Full-device VPN: If a full-device VPN is active, Private Relay may be disabled, or Private Relay traffic may route through the VPN depending on OS behavior. On iOS, system tends to favor a single active network tunnel. For predictable full-device protection, a VPN is more preferred.

DNS configurations: If you manually configured private DNS or custom resolver settings, Private Relay may not be able to route DNS as expected for Safari. In particular, some custom DNS or local filtering may conflict with Private Relay's operation.

Multiple browsers: iCloud Private Relay protects Safari. If you use Chrome or Firefox, consider their own DoH/DoT options and/or a VPN for full-device coverage.

7.10 Private Relay privacy & security analysis

Strong points:

- Eliminates single-point-of-failure confidentiality (no one entity sees both user identity and destination).

- Default integration: Apple manages infrastructure and experience, making it easy for non-technical users to get improved privacy without configuring more complex tools.

Remaining risks:

- Relays (ingress/egress) still see partial data (IP or destination). Adversaries with legal or technical control over both relays could, in theory, correlate data. Apple's architecture asserts independence between the two operators.

- Coverage is limited to Safari—apps can still leak data via other channels (cookies, account logins, analytics).

- Apple's policy and technical implementation may change; users must remain aware of Apple's privacy statements and third-party audits (if any).

7.11 Practical tips & recommended settings

- Use iCloud Private Relay for daily Safari browsing, and pair with good browser hygiene: use a password manager (e.g. iCloud Keychain), use tracker blockers, and use privacy-respecting search engines when desired.

- If you need full-device protection (all apps), choose a trusted VPN with a clear no-logs policy (ideally audited)— and prefer modern protocols (WireGuard or OpenVPN). Alternatively, you can build your own VPN. See Chapter 3 for more details.

- Do not rely on Private Relay alone if you have high anonymity needs: combine with or switch to Tor where necessary.

- Performance: If a site requires location-specific content (e.g. local news), set Private Relay's IP location to "Maintain general location". If you want a higher degree of location obfuscation, pick "Use country and time zone".

- When troubleshooting connectivity: Temporarily disable VPNs, custom DNS, ad-blocking proxies, and network profiles to isolate the problem.

7.12 FAQ: Quick answers

Q: Does Private Relay hide my browsing from Apple?
A: Not fully: Apple's ingress relay sees source IPs but not destination; a separate egress operator sees destination but not source. The split-trust model is designed so Apple cannot see both at once.

Q: Does Private Relay work on Wi-Fi and cellular?
A: Yes (if your carrier/network doesn't block it and your iCloud+ subscription is active).

Q: Will Private Relay slow down browsing?
A: Typically not noticeably for regular web browsing, but it may add latency compared to direct connections. Tor will generally be slower; some VPNs may be faster or slower depending on protocol/server.

Q: Can I use Private Relay and a VPN at the same time?
A: In most cases, system-level VPNs will override or disable Private Relay. The behavior can vary; test and select the tool that fits your coverage needs.

Q: Is Private Relay available worldwide?

A: It's available broadly but may be restricted or disabled in certain regions or on managed corporate networks.

7.13 Closing notes

Apple's iCloud Private Relay is a thoughtful, easy-to-use privacy tool that raises the baseline privacy for millions of Safari users. Its split-relay architecture is especially attractive for users who prefer not to put complete trust in a single VPN operator—and for those who want a frictionless improvement in privacy without installing third-party software. However, Private Relay is not a full replacement for a VPN. Use it for everyday safe browsing on Apple devices, and combine it with a system VPN for other traffic or when higher anonymity is needed.

8 Tor: Overview, Setup, and Practical Use

This chapter explains what Tor is, how onion routing works, and the common use cases and limits. It provides step-by-step, platform-specific tutorials for installing and using the Tor Browser (Windows, macOS, Linux, Android, iOS), explains how to configure and use bridges and pluggable transports (e.g. obfs4), and for advanced users, how to publish a simple onion service.

Note: Tor provides strong anonymity properties when used correctly, but no system gives perfect anonymity. Tor protects routing metadata by design; application-level leaks (e.g. logging in to a personal account) can deanonymize you. Always keep Tor Browser updated and follow recommended hardening steps. For official Tor resources, downloads, and documentation, see the Tor Project.

8.1 What is Tor?

Tor (The Onion Router) is a free, volunteer-run overlay network that helps users preserve anonymity online by routing traffic through a series of encrypted relays so that no single relay knows both the origin and destination of a stream. Tor is implemented and distributed by the Tor Project and is widely used for privacy, censorship circumvention, secure research, and other legitimate uses.

- **How Tor works (brief):** Your Tor client picks a random path of (typically) three relays—an entry (guard) node, a middle node, and an exit node. Each hop knows only its predecessor and successor. Data is layered with encryption ("onion" layers); each relay peels one layer and forwards the rest, so no single node sees both source IP and destination.

- **Key properties:** helps hide which sites you visit from your ISP; helps hide your IP from destination sites; provides access to .onion (hidden) services that are only reachable inside the Tor network.

For more information about the Tor Project (e.g. what Tor is and why it exists), see the Tor Project website (https://www.torproject.org).

8.2 When to use Tor: Benefits and limits

- **Use Tor when:** you need strong anonymity (activists, journalists, researchers in repressive environments), to bypass network censorship, or to access onion services.

- **Don't count on Tor for:** high bandwidth tasks (large downloads or HD video streaming—Tor is slow compared with direct connections), or for protecting data after you log into identifying accounts (e.g. your personal Google account). Tor hides routing, not content you provide to a site when you authenticate.

- **Threat model reminder:** Tor protects routing-level anonymity. A compromised endpoint (malware), browser fingerprinting, or login sessions that tie to your real-world identity can defeat anonymity.

For a comparison among Tor, Private Relay and VPNs, and to help decide which tool is appropriate for your goals, see Chapter 9, Private Relay vs. VPN and Tor.

8.3 Tor Browser: Install and first steps

8.3.1 Get the Tor Browser

Official source: Always download Tor Browser from the Tor Project website to avoid tampered builds. Official downloads and signatures are on the Tor Project download page.

8.3.2 Windows: GUI install and first run

1. Open your browser and go to `https://www.torproject.org/download/`. Verify checksums/signatures if you are able to.

2. Click **Download for Windows**, save and run the installer.

3. Follow the install wizard, choose install location, then click **Finish** when done.

4. Launch Tor Browser from Start Menu. On first run Tor Browser shows a "Connect" screen (or a "Configure" option if you are behind a restrictive network/in need of bridges).

5. Click **Connect** to automatically connect to the Tor network; or click **Configure** to set up bridges/pluggable transports if your network blocks Tor. (See section on Bridges below)

Note for power users (Windows WSL / sysadmins): Tor Browser is intended to be used via its GUI. If you need a system-wide Tor daemon on Windows for applications that support SOCKS proxies, you can run a Windows build of tor (advanced) but follow Tor Project instructions for signatures and safe configuration. Always prefer the Tor Browser bundle for web browsing.

8.3.3 macOS

1. Visit Tor Project download page and get the macOS build.

2. Open the downloaded `.dmg` file and drag Tor Browser.app to `/Applications`.

3. Open Tor Browser.app (you may need to allow the app in Security & Privacy for first launch). Use the same **Connect / Configure** options described above.

8.3.4 Linux (Ubuntu/Debian example)

Option 1: GUI bundle (recommended): Download `tor-browser-linux64-*.tar.xz` from Tor Project, extract, and run `start-tor-browser.desktop`. Example:

```
# Example: Extract and start Tor Browser
# in user space
tar -xvf tor-browser-linux64-*.tar.xz
cd tor-browser_en-US
./start-tor-browser.desktop
```

Option 2: `torbrowser-launcher` (Ubuntu): A helper that downloads and configures Tor Browser for you:

```
sudo apt update
sudo apt install torbrowser-launcher
torbrowser-launcher
```

Note: `torbrowser-launcher` downloads the official Tor Browser bundle and verifies signatures. Confirm the package source and signature before installing.

8.3.5 Android

Tor Browser for Android is an official app and is available on Google Play and as an APK from the Tor Project. Use the Play Store listing to install, or get the APK from the Tor Project website.

8.3.6 iOS

There is no official Tor Browser for iOS, at the time of writing. The Tor Project recommends iOS apps such as **Onion Browser** and **Orbot** for Tor access on iOS. Because Apple requires browsers on iOS to use WebKit, iOS browser apps cannot implement the same privacy protections as Tor Browser on desktop. Refer to the Tor Project's guidance for iOS.

8.4 Bridges and pluggable transports

When a network (ISP, national firewall) blocks access to the Tor network, you can use **bridges** and **pluggable transports** to hide Tor traffic and get connected. Tor provides multiple transport options (obfs4 is commonly used). The Tor Browser connection settings include a "Use a bridge" toggle and options to input bridge lines.

8.4.1 Bridges: Step-by-step (Tor Browser)

1. Open Tor Browser → Click **Configure** on the initial connection dialog (or open Preferences → Tor → Connection Settings).

2. Select **Yes** when asked if your connection is censored.

3. Choose **Use a bridge**. Select from provided bridge types:

   o **obfs4**: The most widely recommended pluggable transport for censorship circumvention.

   o **meek**: Masquerades traffic in CDN/HTTPS requests (useful where obfs4 is blocked or when you need domain fronting-like behavior).

4. Either select "Request a bridge from torproject.org" (Tor will try to fetch bridges) or **Obtain a bridge line** from the Tor Project's bridge request page, email, or the Tor Project's bridge distribution channels, and paste the bridge string into the provided box.

5. Click **Connect**. If that bridge fails, try another bridge line or transport.

8.4.2 Advanced: Using obfs4proxy with a system Tor

For advanced users only: If you run `tor` as a system daemon and want to use obfs4, confirm `obfs4proxy` is installed and add bridge lines to the `torrc`. Example:

```
# Example torrc entries (system /etc/tor/torrc)
ClientTransportPlugin obfs4 exec /usr/bin/obfs4proxy
```

```
Bridge obfs4 <bridge_address> <bridge_fingerprint>
cert=<cert> iat-mode=0
UseBridges 1
```

After editing `torrc`, reload or restart Tor:

```
sudo systemctl restart tor
sudo journalctl -u tor -f
```

Note: Only use bridges that you obtain from official distribution channels.

8.5 Hardening Tor Browser & best practices

- **Always use the Tor Browser bundle for browsing, not regular browsers configured to use Tor:** The Tor Browser includes multiple hardening patches and privacy features (resists fingerprinting, isolates first/third-party assets, includes HTTPS-First policies, etc.).

- **Block plugins and external helpers:** Do not install browser plugins (Flash, Java, or arbitrary extensions) into Tor Browser; they can leak data or defeat protections.

- **Disable scripts only if needed:** Tor Browser ships with security slider options. JavaScript increases functionality but can increase fingerprint surface. Use the Security Level slider to increase protections (disable JavaScript on the highest setting).

- **Be careful with downloads:** Opening downloaded files (PDFs, Office docs) outside Tor Browser can call external helpers that connect outside Tor and leak your real IP. If you must handle a file, open it in an isolated environment (a disposable VM or Tails) and prefer "view in the browser" where possible.

- **Use bridges with pluggable transports to avoid local censorship.**

- **Keep Tor Browser updated.** The Tor Project regularly releases security updates and fixes.

8.6 Tails: Live OS that ships Tor by default

If you need a disposable, privacy-focused environment, consider Tails—The Amnesic Incognito Live System—a live Linux distribution that routes all network traffic through Tor and does not persist data unless explicitly configured. Tails is useful for high-risk environments and for opening sensitive files in an isolated session. Refer to the Tails website (https://tails.net) for download and installation instructions.

8.7 Advanced: Running an onion (hidden) service

Advanced users can run an onion (hidden) service. Onion services let you host services reachable only within the Tor network (addresses ending in .onion). This example shows a minimal HTTP onion service on Linux.

What you'll host (example)

- A small static site served by nginx on localhost port 8080.

- A Tor hidden service that maps an onion hostname to this local port.

Install Tor and nginx (Debian/Ubuntu example)

```
sudo apt update
sudo apt install tor nginx -y
```

Configure your onion service (edit torrc)

Append to /etc/tor/torrc:

```
HiddenServiceDir /var/lib/tor/hidden_service/
HiddenServiceVersion 3
HiddenServicePort 80 127.0.0.1:8080
```

- HiddenServiceDir will be created by Tor and will contain hostname (your .onion) and private key files.

- HiddenServiceVersion 3 selects modern v3 onion addresses (stronger security than v2). Always use v3 today.

Restart Tor:

```
sudo systemctl restart tor
sudo journalctl -u tor -f
```

Configure nginx (example)

Create /etc/nginx/sites-available/tor-site:

```
server {
    listen 127.0.0.1:8080;
    server_name localhost;

    location / {
        root /var/www/tor-site;
        index index.html;
```

```
        }
}
```

Enable and start nginx:

```
sudo mkdir -p /var/www/tor-site
echo "<h1>Hello from Tor hidden service</h1>" \
  | sudo tee /var/www/tor-site/index.html
sudo ln -s /etc/nginx/sites-available/tor-site \
  /etc/nginx/sites-enabled/
sudo systemctl restart nginx
```

Retrieve your onion hostname

After Tor creates the hidden service directory, read the hostname:

```
sudo cat /var/lib/tor/hidden_service/hostname
# will print something like: abcde.onion
```

You can now reach your site by visiting the .onion address in Tor Browser (desktop or mobile). The address is only resolvable via Tor.

8.8 Troubleshooting & Diagnostics

- **Tor Browser won't connect?** Try **Configure → Use a bridge** and test obfs4; check your network for firewall rules blocking port 9001 or 9030 (ORPort/DirPort). Check the Tor logs (View the Tor Network Settings or Browser Console).

- **Tor is slow?** Tor is designed for anonymity, not speed. Use the network when needed; avoid streaming large media.

81

- **My onion service doesn't resolve?** Confirm HiddenServiceDir exists and Tor restarted after changes. Look for errors in `/var/log/tor` or `journalctl -u tor`.

8.9 Closing notes

Tor is a powerful tool when used correctly and combined with careful operational security. This chapter gave you the conceptual background, practical install steps for major platforms, configuration steps for bridges and pluggable transports, Tor Browser hardening suggestions, and a basic onion service walkthrough.

For more information and advanced topics (e.g. custom Tor deployments, integrating Tor with other privacy tools, or running production onion services), consult the Tor Project (https://www.torproject.org) website's documentation and community resources.

9 Private Relay vs. VPN and Tor

In this chapter, we compare Apple's iCloud Private Relay with VPN and Tor and explore practical examples and scenarios.

9.1 Private Relay vs. VPN

A VPN encrypts *all* your network traffic and changes your apparent location as chosen on the VPN server. Private Relay only covers Safari. VPNs require trust in the provider (it sees your traffic and real IP). Private Relay splits trust (Apple doesn't know your site, and CDN partner doesn't know you). Both use strong encryption. VPNs can use any port (often UDP) and work for all apps. Private Relay is over HTTPS (TCP 443) and only Safari. If you need an IP from a specific country or want all apps covered, a VPN is better. If you only want Safari privacy and trust Apple's implementation, Private Relay is convenient and built in.

9.2 Private Relay vs. Tor

Tor routes your traffic through at least 3 nodes; it hides your IP very well. Private Relay is only 2 hops (Apple and one partner). Tor is more anonymous (no central provider, volunteer network, also hides metadata), but often slower. Use Tor Browser for robust anonymity; use Private Relay for moderate privacy without Tor's complexity. Private Relay does not anonymize you from websites in the same way Tor does—it merely hides your exact IP.

9.3 Comparison tables: Private Relay vs. VPN and Tor

9.3.1 Table A: Feature & UX comparison

Feature / Property	Private Relay (iCloud+)	VPN (commercial or self-hosted)
Coverage (what traffic)	Safari (and some system DNS) only	Whole device (all apps) when enabled
Ease of use	Very easy (system toggle)	Easy with apps; medium for manual setup
Server selection (choose country)	No (region-level only)	Yes—many providers, choose exit country
Trust model	Split-trust: Apple + third-party egress	Single provider (you must trust VPN operator)
Logging risk	Reduced due to split-relay; limited logs at each hop	Depends on provider & jurisdiction (some log)
Performance (latency & speed)	Generally low overhead (fast for browsing)	Varies—WireGuard is fast; OpenVPN moderate
Cost	Included with iCloud+ subscription	Free (self-hosted) to subscription fees

Feature / Property	Private Relay (iCloud+)	VPN (commercial or self-hosted)
Bypasses geoblocks	Limited (no country-selection)	Yes—full country/server selection
Works on public Wi-Fi	Yes for Safari	Yes for all traffic
Protects against ISP DNS logging	Yes for Safari DNS	Yes (if VPN pushes DNS)
Use-case fit	Everyday browsing privacy on Apple devices	Full-device privacy, regional access

Feature / Property	Tor (Tor Browser / Tor network)
Coverage (what traffic)	Tor Browser apps (only traffic via Tor Browser / configured apps)
Ease of use	Moderate to complex (use Tor Browser for easiest)
Server selection (choose country)	No control of specific exit node; can set exit preferences with risk
Trust model	Decentralized, volunteer-run relays (no single trusted operator)
Logging risk	Low if using official Tor network (but exit nodes see destination traffic)
Performance (latency & speed)	Slowest (multiple hops, volunteer relays)

Feature / Property	Tor (Tor Browser / Tor network)
Cost	Free (Tor network)
Bypasses geoblocks	Sometimes; exit node geo may help but unreliable for streaming
Works on public Wi-Fi	Yes, but slow and some networks block Tor
Protects against ISP DNS logging	Yes (Tor resolves via Tor network)
Use-case fit	High anonymity, censorship circumvention (with speed tradeoffs)

9.3.2 Table B: Privacy / Threat-model comparison

Threat / Goal	Private Relay	VPN
Hide browsing from local network/ISP (Safari)	Yes (designed for this)	Yes (if all traffic via VPN)
Avoid central provider seeing both who and what	Designed for this (split-relay)	No (provider sees both origin & destination)
Resist strong global adversary (e.g. nation-state)	Limited—provides protection against casual observers, but not guaranteed against powerful	Depends—VPN provider could be compelled; self-hosting reduces some risks

Threat / Goal	Private Relay	VPN
	adversaries or those controlling both relays	
Protect all apps & leak vectors	No—Safari only	Yes if full-device VPN
Defend against fingerprinting or tracking-by-login	Limited (helps with IP hiding)	Limited (hiding IP helps; cookies / fingerprinting remain)
Log-less guarantee	Partial—split relays limit data each holds; depends on operators	Varies—depends on provider policy & audits

Threat / Goal	Tor
Hide browsing from local network/ISP (Safari)	Yes (Tor circuits hide origin)
Avoid central provider seeing both who and what	Yes (distributed relays; no single party sees both ends)
Resist strong global adversary (e.g. nation-state)	Better—Tor's decentralization reduces single-point compromise, though correlation attacks are possible
Protect all apps & leak vectors	Only Tor Browser or configured apps

Threat / Goal	Tor
Defend against fingerprinting or tracking-by-login	Better when combined with Tor Browser's anti-fingerprinting measures
Log-less guarantee	High—no central logs (but exit nodes can see content if not encrypted)

9.4 Practical examples & scenarios

Scenario 1: Everyday user on public Wi-Fi

- Goal: Prevent the cafe Wi-Fi operator or hotspot snooper from seeing the exact websites visited in Safari.

- Recommended: Enable iCloud Private Relay (simple, automatic). If you need to protect all apps, use a reputable or self-hosted VPN instead.

Scenario 2: Need to access region-locked streaming content

- Goal: Make a service think you are in another country.

- Recommended: Use VPN with a server in the target country (Private Relay cannot choose country-level exit beyond limited region options).

Scenario 3: Journalists/activists requiring robust anonymity

- Goal: High anonymity and resistance to powerful adversaries.

- Recommended: Use Tor Browser and follow advanced Tor operational security guidance (avoid logging into personal accounts, avoid plugins that deanonymize, etc.).

In summary, you should choose the right tool for your goals:

- For daily Safari privacy on Apple devices: Private Relay is an excellent option.

- For full-device coverage (all apps), geographic server selection, or streaming needs: Use a VPN.

- For robust anonymity and censorship circumvention: Use Tor (with careful operational security).

10 Artificial Intelligence (AI) and Privacy

As artificial intelligence (AI) features proliferate, we must also consider privacy in that context. Many modern apps integrate AI (voice assistants, generative AI, on-device intelligence). In this chapter, we cover important principles and examples.

10.1 On-device AI vs. cloud AI

A key distinction is whether AI processing happens *on the device* or in the cloud. **On-device AI** means your data doesn't leave your hardware: only results (or very limited data) are sent elsewhere. Apple champions this approach: Their Apple Intelligence (Siri, image recognition, etc.) runs on the device by default. For complex tasks, they use a "Private Cloud Compute" that sends only the minimal data needed, and supposedly does not store your personal information.

Samsung has a similar stance with its Galaxy AI (on newer Galaxy phones). They promote on-device tools like Live Translate, Audio Eraser, etc., that keep "inputs... within the confines of your phone". Even cloud-based features, Samsung says, do not store data long-term or use it for training: "personal data is never stored long-term or used for AI training". They allow users to disable online processing if desired. In 2023, Google also announced on-device transcription on Pixel phones.

In summary, there is a trend where newer devices aim to do more AI locally, or at least minimize what's sent to the cloud. As users, we can prefer on-device AI features over cloud AI for increased privacy.

10.2 Generative AI tools

When using generative AI tools such as ChatGPT and Bard, users must be cautious:

- **Data retention:** Many chatbot services log your prompts and responses for quality/training purposes unless you opt out. For example, OpenAI now says users can *opt out* of having their data used for training, and can delete conversations entirely. Always check "Data Controls" in the app (e.g. in ChatGPT's settings).

- **Private mode:** Some apps or extensions provide an "incognito" mode. For instance, DuckDuckGo's Duck.ai chat runs behind the scenes and does not log queries for training, storing conversations only on your device. It emphasizes optional and private AI: "AI features are optional and can be turned off". If privacy is critical, use such tools or the "anonymous proxy" chats like Duck.ai.

- **Local LLMs:** Recently, AI models such as OpenAI's GPT-4o and Meta's Llama can run in a lightweight mode on-device. These are evolving fields. The advantage is your data never leaves the device.

- **General advice:** Don't paste sensitive info into AI chats. Always use HTTPS and, if available, browser isolation. Some services (like Google Workspace) have privacy guarantees that enterprise data isn't used to train models, which may help in certain use cases.

10.3 AI in smart devices and voice assistants

Smart devices and voice assistants (e.g. Alexa, Google Assistant, Siri) raise some privacy concerns:

- **Wake word buffers:** Some voice assistants record continuously and only send data after the "wake word" is detected. Others buffer all audio temporarily. It is important to know how long data is being stored.

- **Reviewing recordings:** You can usually review and delete voice recordings in your account (Amazon, Google, Apple) as a privacy practice.

- **On-device vs. cloud:** Siri and Google's recent improvements have moved more recognition on-device, reducing the amount of audio data being sent. Check if your device has a "On-device voice recognition" setting (e.g. Google Pixel Recorder's speech-to-text is on-device by default).

- **Alexa and Ring:** If you use Amazon devices, remember Alexa can store transcripts. Make sure to prune voice history regularly.

- **Privacy modes:** Many assistants have a way to turn off always-listening (e.g. push a mic off button or say "Alexa, turn off microphone").

In summary, treat AI assistants like any other always-on device: minimize exposure by disabling them when not needed, and use secure (on-device) features where possible.

11 Looking Ahead: AI-powered Privacy: Intelligent Defenses

Looking ahead to the future, artificial intelligence (AI) can significantly enhance your online privacy when integrated with technologies such as virtual private networks (VPNs). For example, AI can enhance your online privacy by making VPNs smarter, more adaptive, and proactive. It doesn't just shield your IP—it actively analyzes threats, adapts protections, and helps you make informed choices about your digital safety.

Below are several key mechanisms through which AI can work with VPNs and other tools to boost privacy.

11.1 Intelligent server selection and traffic optimization

Traditional VPNs route your traffic through a fixed server or a manually chosen server location. AI takes this further by:

- **Analyzing latency and load in real time**: An AI model monitors server response times, current bandwidth usage, and packet-loss statistics across hundreds of endpoints. When you connect, the system chooses the "optimal" server that offers both strong encryption and minimal slowdown.

- **Dynamic load balancing**: If a chosen VPN exit node begins to experience congestion or unusual spikes in traffic, AI can instantly switch your connection to a

93

healthier node without you noticing, thereby maintaining both speed and privacy.

Why it matters:
Faster, more reliable connections reduce the temptation to disable the VPN. AI's continual adjustments discourage you from "VPN-ping-ponging" (disconnecting and reconnecting to a different server) or disabling encryption altogether— common user behaviors that degrade privacy.

11.2 Real-time anomaly and threat detection

Even when your traffic is encrypted, endpoints or DNS requests can leak information. AI enhances detection of suspicious activity by:

- **Profile-based traffic analysis**: Machine learning models "learn" your typical usage patterns—times of day you stream, websites you visit, protocols you use (e.g. HTTPS vs. plain HTTP). If a sudden, unexplained DNS lookup or IP packet pattern emerges, the AI flags it.

- **Automatic blocklists and reputation systems**: AI systems continuously ingest threat-intelligence feeds (malicious IP addresses, phishing domains, known malware C&C servers). They cross-reference your outgoing requests in real time; if your local device tries to call out to a domain on the blocklist, the VPN client can automatically refuse or reroute that DNS query.

Why it matters:
Many privacy leaks don't come from your physical location— they come from "invisible" calls your browser or apps make in

the background. AI sees those "noisy" signals faster than a static rule-based firewall ever could, preventing data leaks or tracking cookies from creeping through.

11.3 Adaptive encryption strength

Most VPNs default to a single encryption cipher (e.g. AES-256). AI allows for **context-aware encryption** by:

- **Assessing network environment** (public Wi-Fi vs. home network vs. work network).

- **Evaluating real-time threat levels** (for example, if the user is accessing financial sites or sensitive platforms).

- **Modulating cipher suite**:

  - On a coffee-shop Wi-Fi, AI might enforce AES-256 with SHA-512 hashing and a fresh ephemeral key on each session.

  - At home—where the router is known and hardware security is high—the AI could permit AES-128 to reduce CPU usage and save battery on mobile devices.

Why it matters:
You get maximal privacy when it's most critical, and reasonable performance at lower risk. Static VPN clients can't make those trade-offs in real time: you either run maximal encryption all the time (draining battery and CPU) or run a weaker cipher to save resources.

11.4 Automated "kill switch" and connection repair

A "kill switch" halts all internet traffic if your VPN tunnel collapses unexpectedly—preventing an unencrypted "leak". AI improves this by:

- **Predicting dropouts**: By monitoring signal quality, jitter, and packet-loss trends, an AI model can often foresee an impending disconnect (e.g. you're leaving the Wi-Fi range). The client can then proactively shift to the next best network (cellular data, another Wi-Fi) without ever exposing your real IP.

- **Instant recovery**: If a drop does occur, AI orchestrates a mini "re-negotiation" of encryption parameters and rapidly reopens a secure tunnel—often faster than a human would notice.

Why it matters:
Even a few seconds of downtime can expose your true IP or DNS. AI's proactive monitoring makes sure you stay behind an encrypted tunnel 100% of the time.

11.5 Personalized privacy presets

AI can learn your habits—websites you visit, the applications you run, times of day you work, etc.—and then:

- **Auto-enable/disable the VPN** for specific apps or domains.

  - When you open your banking app, the VPN is forced on.

- When you stream a geo-restricted video, it auto-selects a server in the correct country.

- **Adaptive ad and tracker blocking**.

  - If you frequently hit news sites that embed dozens of third-party trackers, the AI can match those domain calls against a curated privacy list and selectively block trackers at the DNS or HTTP layer.

- **Suggesting privacy score improvements**.

  - You might get a weekly "Privacy Report" telling you: "You accessed 7 new third-party trackers this week—consider enabling 'aggressive tracker blocking' when you visit these domains."

Why it matters:
Rather than forcing you to memorize dozens of switches and toggles, AI "owns" the complexity. You simply choose a broad privacy level (e.g. "Work," "Streaming," "Financial"), and the system configures itself.

11.6 Machine-learning-driven DNS privacy

Even with a VPN, DNS leaks can reveal which websites you're visiting. AI enhances DNS privacy via:

- **Encrypted DNS query routing** (DNS over HTTPS/TLS), where the AI dynamically picks the fastest, most secure resolver.

- **Predictive prefetching**: By observing your behavior —"every morning at 8 AM you check example-bank.com"—the AI can prefetch DNS entries in advance over an encrypted channel, reducing latency without touching your actual browsing.

- **Smart fallback**: If the primary encrypted resolver goes down, AI instantly switches to a secondary encrypted resolver (e.g. from Cloudflare's 1.1.1.1 to Google's 8.8.8.8 over DoT) with no unencrypted "fail open".

Why it matters:
Encrypted DNS isn't just about hiding "which domains" you query; it's also about ensuring that your DNS requests aren't logged or sold. AI's continuous monitoring of resolver health reduces the chance that you'll "fall back" to an unencrypted lookup.

11.7 Threat intelligence and AI-driven blocklists

VPN providers increasingly subscribe to global threat-intelligence feeds—continuously updated lists of:

- Malicious IP ranges (botnets, spam distributors)

- Newly registered phishing or malware domains

- Known "fingerprinting" or "tracking" servers

AI ingests these feeds in real time, correlates them with any local telemetry (failed connection attempts, odd-looking SSL certificates), and blocks or quarantines suspicious endpoints:

- **Local DNS sinkhole**: If an app attempts to connect to a known tracking domain, the AI can rewrite that DNS request to `0.0.0.0`, effectively null-routing it.

- **Proactive warning**: When you try to visit a site listed in the phishing database, the AI could alert you with a "Warning: Suspicious site—proceed?" dialog before loading.

Why it matters:
Static blocklists become obsolete within days. AI continually curates, prunes, and prioritizes which entries matter most for you—reducing false positives while ensuring genuinely malicious domains never slip through.

11.8 Behavioral fingerprint hardening

Even behind a VPN, websites can piece together a browser "fingerprint" (screen size, OS version, installed fonts, etc.) to track you. AI can help by:

- **Detecting fingerprint-harvesting scripts**: Machine learning models scan a website's JavaScript on the fly. If they recognize code patterns used for canvas-fingerprinting or font enumeration, they either block or sandbox those scripts.

- **Noise injection**: In cases where blocking is impossible, AI injects subtle, randomized "noise" into the fingerprint. For example, it might slightly tweak your reported timezone or randomize canvas output—enough to break fingerprint consistency, yet not enough to break site functionality.

Why it matters:
A VPN hides your IP address, but fingerprinting can tie together multiple sessions anyway. AI's real-time detection and mitigation of fingerprint collectors seals that loophole.

11.9 Continuous privacy auditing and reporting

Finally, AI can produce ongoing "privacy audits" in the background:

- **Leak detection reports**: Every week, an AI script checks whether your IP or DNS has ever "leaked" by comparing logs from external auditing services.

- **Usage summaries**: "You spent 5 hours streaming video this week. We noticed 12 different trackers on the streaming site—would you like to enable more aggressive tracker blocking next time?"

- **Privacy score**: Based on your behaviors (e.g. how often you jump networks, how many third-party trackers you encounter, how many times your VPN disconnected unexpectedly), AI assigns you a "Privacy Score" out of 100. Over time, it recommends specific changes (e.g. "Switch your VPN to 'always-on' mode for mobile" or "Upgrade to an AI-powered DNS service with malware filtering").

Why it matters:
Most people remain oblivious to subtle leaks of personal information. AI's continuous analysis and digestible reports educate users, nudging them to adopt better habits, resulting in lasting improvements to their privacy posture.

11.10 Closing notes

Looking ahead to the future, by combining a VPN's core strengths (IP masking, encrypted tunnels) with AI's adaptive, real-time intelligence, you can get a privacy solution that:

- **Stays ahead of emerging threats** (zero-day phishing domains, novel fingerprinting techniques).

- **Optimizes performance vs. security** (stronger encryption only when needed).

- **Reduces manual configuration** (personalized, automated presets).

- **Blocks hidden trackers** (adaptive DNS blocking, script detection).

- **Ensures continuous protection** (smart kill switches, automatic server failover).

In essence, AI could transform a VPN or similar technology from a static "tunnel" into a proactive, self-tuning privacy guardian—one that learns from your habits, reacts to emerging threats, and optimizes itself without constant user intervention. The result is a seamless, high-confidence privacy experience that's far more robust than either a VPN or AI alone could deliver.

Conclusion: Building Your Privacy Toolbox in the Age of AI

In this book, we've explored the **breadth of modern privacy tools**:

- **Encryption (VPN, Tor, encrypted DNS)** to shield your traffic from eavesdroppers and hide your identity.

- **Anonymization (Tor, iCloud Private Relay)** to prevent linking you to your actions.

- **Local controls (browser, OS settings)** to limit data collection on your own device.

- **Service choices (DNS providers, search engines, AI tools)** that respect privacy by policy or design.

- **AI-powered privacy with intelligent defenses** for a seamless, high-confidence and robust privacy experience.

No single solution "solves" privacy, but by combining layers, you can protect yourself under many scenarios. For example, a common stack: Use a VPN or Private Relay for IP anonymity; enable encrypted DNS or DNSCrypt to hide lookups; browse with a hardened browser (Firefox with uBlock Origin or containers, or Safari with Intelligent Tracking Prevention (ITP)); and limit app permissions at the OS level. This covers the network, application, and OS layers. Combine these with AI-powered privacy with intelligent defenses for a seamless experience.

As technology evolves (5G, IoT, new AI features), the privacy landscape shifts. Always stay informed: New OS versions and devices often add privacy features (e.g. Android Privacy Sandbox, iOS Lockdown mode). The principles remain: **minimize shared data** and **encrypt what you can**.

Remember: Privacy is a continuous process, not a one-time setup. Review your tools periodically, update software, and adapt to new threats (e.g. if Apple changes how Private Relay works, or if a browser tracking scheme emerges). Your effort pays off in keeping your digital life secure and private.

Stay safe, stay private, and take control of your online world.

About the Author

Lin Song, PhD, is a Software Engineer and open source developer. He created and maintains the Setup IPsec VPN projects on GitHub since 2014, for building your own VPN server in just a few minutes. The projects have 20,000+ GitHub stars and 30 million+ Docker pulls, and have helped millions of users set up their own VPN servers.

Connect with Lin Song
Amazon: https://amazon.com/author/linsong
GitHub: https://github.com/hwdsl2
LinkedIn: https://www.linkedin.com/in/linsongui

Thanks for reading! I do hope you get the best from reading this book. If this book was helpful to you, I'd be very grateful if you leave a rating or post a short review.

Thanks,
Lin Song
Author

www.ingramcontent.com/pod-product-compliance
Lightning Source LLC
Chambersburg PA
CBHW071718210326
41597CB00017B/2522